RUBY'S DANCE

One Woman's Motorcycle Journey
Across North America

Mary Jane Stein

To my Mom
Thank you for always supporting me
in whatever I decided to do,
even when you thought it was not the best idea.

To all the people I met on this journey
I am so grateful for your kindness and your laughter,
Thank you for being part of my life.

CONTENTS

Title Page

Dedication

Preface

Part I: Vancouver, B.C. to Zealand, New Brunswick   1

Part II: The Maritimes   38

Part III: Yarmouth, N.S. to Vancouver, B.C.   82

Part IV: What did I Learn From this Journey?   139

About The Author   145

PREFACE

I'm always daunted by a journal's blank pages
but I have something I need to say:

There's a dance that happens between me and the Universe
when I ride my bike.
Mostly it happens in the curves;
You let go of the throttle a bit as you're coming in and eye it up,
Just as you're leaning in before the apex,
you throttle up and counter steer.

And Ruby glides through the curve
Like she's flying, like I'm flying,
Like the road is a thing of beauty
meant to be flown on.
The momentum of the curve
shoots you out the other side; Synergy.

The power of the bike and the power of the curve,
Aligned in perfect sync.
That's the dance.

PART I: VANCOUVER, B.C. TO ZEALAND, NEW BRUNSWICK

Map 1: Vancouver BC
to Zealand NB

#1. North Vancouver BC
#2. Greenwood BC: Day 1
#3. Balfour BC: Day 2-3
#4. Fernie BC: Day 4
#5. Kalispell MT: Day 5-6
#6. Havre MT: Day 7
#7. Williston ND: Day 8
#8. Arvilla ND: Day 9
#9. Grand Rapids MN: Day 10
#10. Prentice WI: Day 11
#11. Manistique MI: Day 12
#12. Pinconning MI: Day 13
#13. Brighton MI: Day 14-16
#14. Milton ONT: Day 17
#15. Johnstown ONT: Day 18
#16. Levis QUE: Day 19
#17. Grand Falls NB: Day 20
#18. Zealand NB: Day 21

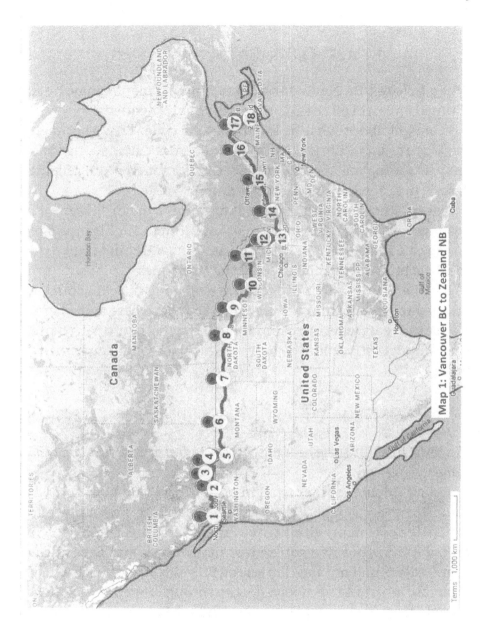

Map 1: Vancouver BC to Zealand NB

Seven Days Before Leaving

When I visited Dr. Nevin for a dental appointment today, he exclaimed, "Wow! You're taking your bike across Canada!"

I thought about what he said for a long time. That's not really the way it is. I'm not taking my bike across Canada – my bike, Ruby, is taking me across Canada – that's a much more accurate description of what's really happening.

I don't know exactly where I'm going. I mean, I know I'm heading east. I know I want to visit my Mom in Michigan and my youngest daughter Kat in Nova Scotia. I know I would like to ride the Cape Breton Trail and explore the Maritimes.

But there will be lots of decisions every day that I'm counting on Ruby to help me make: which road to take, where and when to stop for a break, where to camp at night or whether to get a motel. Most importantly, I need to be aware of when to talk and when to listen.

Five Days Before Leaving

In a James Taylor song he sings, *It's OK to feel afraid. Just don't let it stand in your way.*

I'm afraid about this trip. I'm afraid it will be hard to find a campsite even though I've always been able to find a place for my little tent on previous trips. I'm scared I'll get lost, which I probably will, but I've gotten lost many times and have always eventually found my way. I'm scared I'll get wet and tired, which I probably will, but I've always gotten through that before too. I'm scared I'll meet creepy people even though I always meet incredibly amazing people.

You know what? I think I will be just fine; *She believed she could do it, so she did!*

Four Days Before Leaving

I'm not sure if people think I'm crazy. I hesitate to tell anyone I'm riding to Nova Scotia. It's interesting – some people think it's the coolest idea ever and some think it's absolutely nuts. And others think it's kind of both. Yes, it's nuts, but it's also the coolest idea ever.

It's important to prove to myself that I'm strong enough to do this. I don't need to prove it to anyone else. It's like that cliff by the swimming hole between Princeton and Merritt. I had to jump off it just because it was there; I knew I would regret it if I didn't go for it.

That's what this is like . . . all of Canada is out there just waiting for me to experience it from coast to coast. I just want to do it!

One Day Before Leaving

Legends say that Hummingbirds float free of time, carrying our hopes for love, joy and celebration. The Hummingbird's delicate grace reminds us that life is rich, beauty is everywhere, that every personal connection has meaning, and that laughter is life's sweetest creation.

Ruby is a hummingbird. It's like she's taking me on a journey – physical, mental, spiritual, and emotional. What will I discover? Maybe myself. "Be like a little bird," a friend said to me. "Know that you are flying in the right direction."

DAY 1: July 2
North Vancouver to Greenwood, B.C.

Incredibly busy the last few days, trying to clean up my apartment so there's room for my oldest daughter, Mariah and her new husband, Dan the Man, to stay here while I am away for the summer. There's too much unnecessary stuff in my life. Simplify, Mary Jane, simplify your life.

I left this morning with Donna, Razz, and Wendy. We're traveling together to Glacier National Park; then they're going to head back to Vancouver. Donna and I have been neighbors and camping buddies for decades. When our kids grew up and I started riding with Razz and Wendy on road trips, Donna asked, "Maybe I can be your support vehicle? I'd love to camp with you guys!" We said, "Of course!"

It's great to be traveling with these women again. It is so easy to be on the road with them. We never have any arguments about where to stop; never any "hurry up" vibes; just love and laughter and fun. It's easy.

We did 480 km today. We split it into two sections of 150 km, then 100 km, and lastly 80 km. It was good to break the last parts into two smaller pieces because we were all getting tired by the end of the day. We stuck to the speed limit in the last two sections. When you're tired, you want to speed up to reach your destination for the night sooner – but it's not a great idea! Speed + Tiredness = Too easy to make a mistake. A mistake in a car can be a fender bender; a mistake on a bike is almost certainly a serious injury or death. Remember to slow down at the end of the day, Mary Jane.

DAY 2: July 3
Greenwood to Balfour, B.C.

Riding with Wendy and Razz is always such a pleasure. We stick to the speed limit or ten km over (OK, OK, caught in a lie. Sometimes we go twenty over or sometimes thirty over depending on the road, whether we've done it before, road conditions, weather conditions, personal head space, etc.). We switch lead rider every gas stop, so we ride in a different position every 150 km or so. It makes for variety and a change in thinking . . . every position has its own responsibilities.

Arrived at Toad Rock Campground about 5 pm. God, I love this place! You pay for everything on the honor system. You tally up how much you owe at the end of your stay, put the money in an envelope and drop it through the office mail slot. The first time I was here, I tried to pay at the beginning. Mary, the owner laughed at me, "Pay at the end; everybody stays longer than they think they're going to!"

Toad Rock has an open-walled Social Pavilion with a pool table, big screen TV for movies, and Internet. The coffee pot is always on and the beer fridge is full; you serve yourself, put your money in the jar on the counter, and go chat with your new friends. Mary comes around to every campsite in the evening to make sure you feel at home and that you have everything you need. She is an incredibly warm person who has created a truly welcoming place.

DAY 3: July 4
Toad Rock Campground

Had a nice slow morning . . . built a campfire, drank coffee, hung out talking with our camping neighbors, JJ and John. JJ is so funny; he talks a mile a minute, is a machinist, and knows Harley Sportsters like the back of his hand. I've been having trouble with my clutch; Ruby wants to pull forward even with the clutch all the way in. JJ adjusts my clutch cable for me and fills me in on all the ways to get along with a Sportster's persnickety clutch.

Pam and Bernie, also camping neighbors, come over to see what we're working on. Bernie suggests that when the clutch won't disengage enough to shift into neutral, (like when you're trying to back into a parking spot), turn off the engine and then you'll be able to get her into neutral. Voila! Brilliant! We sit and chat for a while. Pam and Bernie are from Golden; they run a campground just outside of town. They're old friends of Mary's and visit Toad Rock whenever they get a chance. Pam rides a Sportster, which is why Bernie understands my temperamental clutch issue.

John is staying in a little cabin next to our campsite. He's older and a very proud war veteran. He seems kind of lonely, so Donna, Razz, Wendy and I have adopted him. He comes over and hangs out at our place most of the time for coffee and companionship. Although he doesn't talk about it, I think he's had a very rough life.

The girls and I go riding today just to explore the surrounding area. Remember the dance? That's what the road between Kaslo and New Denver is made for. It's such a beautiful curvy road with rushing rivers, mountain views and a huge calm lake. The road is like a cruiser ski run: curve, then go up, then down, then curve again, then repeat the whole thing over and over until you're so happy you feel like you're going to burst! We dance our hearts out and then on the way back to Toad Rock we stop at Ainsworth Hot Springs. We warm our bones in the hot mineral water and explore the steaming caves. It's a rush to be all toasty warm and then jump into the ice-cold plunge pool.

I was thinking about how Mary built Toad Rock in the '60s. She focused on ways to construct the camp sites so that people would talk to each other. The toilets and showers are separate and private, but the sinks are communal. You have to drop all your pretensions when you are brushing your teeth next to someone you have never met before. And the kitchen area is communal too. It's open like the Social Pavilion only smaller. There are dishes, pots and pans, a stove, sink and fridge for all your cooking needs. It's a great spot to cook and converse with new friends.

Mary stopped by our campsite as we were eating dinner and asked how our day had been. "It's so fun riding with the girls," I exclaimed happily. "I prefer it to the guys." Mary laughed and replied, "One by day, and one by night!"

DAY 4: July 5
Balfour to Fernie, B.C.

OMG! It took us forever to pack up our camping gear. We ended up chatting with John next door and JJ and Pam and Bernie. Then we went down to the Social Pavilion, talked with Mary and bought Toad Rock T-shirts. After umpteen cups of coffee, we finally hit the road. Took the ferry across Kootenay Lake and stopped in Crawford Bay for lunch and shopping. We checked out a pottery store, a blacksmith shop, a weavers' co-op, and a kiln fired copper jewelry store. How us girls love to shop! We finally put some miles on and arrived in Fernie 300 km later.

Donna had a long talk with me tonight; she's worried about me staying up too late writing in my journal and she's concerned that I'm not getting enough sleep. She's feeling anxious about me continuing on this trip on my own and not taking good care of myself. She's right – getting enough sleep is crucial. Donna quietly suggested that I need to find my own balance to enjoy this journey. I love you Donna – you are such a wise woman. Thank you.

DAY 5: July 6
Fernie, B.C. to Glacier National Park, Kalispell, Montana

Rain and sun . . . rain and sun . . . It's always a smart idea to wear your rain gear in the foothills of the Rockies. The weather changes in a nanosecond. We had a great ride to Glacier National Park, in spite of the rain, but little glitches kept happening. Nothing major, easy to deal with until . . .

We lost each other for two hours in the park. Shit! It shouldn't have happened, for gosh sakes, it was only a fifteen-minute ride from the main gate to our campground. A "clusterfuck" is what Razz called it later. What happened? We got separated; Donna made a wrong turn at the intersection, and Razz went to go find her. Wendy and I went to the first campground. Donna and Razz went to the second campground and then they rode all the way to the third. Total miscommunication and no cell service.

Finally, just as Wendy and I went to look for Donna and Razz, they pulled in. We were all so angry, frustrated, and scared we could hardly speak to each other. We set up camp barely talking. It took a while for all of us (including me) to cool down and realize that we all had contributed to the situation. Each of us could have done something differently that would have created a better result.

Lovely Wendy led us in a cleansing ceremony after dinner. It was exactly what we needed. Smudging, drumming, meditation, and Wendy had made gifts for each of us – soft leather medicine bags to put small treasures in and beaded seed crone necklaces. We are linked together now in spirit … wise women … old crones. I treasure my relationship with these women.

DAY 6: July 7
Glacier National Park, Kalispell, Montana

Darn it all! The Park Ranger made us move campsites. When we got in yesterday, after our clusterfuck, there were no campsites left so they put us in the overflow area. Park regulations say you can camp for only one night in the overflow section. We were hoping that the Park Ranger would take pity on four gorgeous women and let us stay for just one more night in overflow. No such luck; he was blind to our beauty.

We spent almost two and a half hours packing all our gear, moving to a newly vacated site, and setting everything up again. It was actually pretty hilarious; we didn't take the tents down, we just picked them up and walked along the road with them to our new site. We got a lot of laughs from other campers.

We chatted with Matt and Greg, two young men also camping in the overflow area, and like us, forced to move. Matt has a Harley Sportster and Greg has incredible blue eyes, "Enough to make a girl swoon," commented Razz. The guys were both so sweet and gallant last night offering to help us set up camp and sharing their chips and beer in an attempt to cheer us up. We had several good laughs this morning as we all pitched in taking down and setting up camp again in new sites.

The Road to the Sun in Glacier Park is world famous for its numerous switchbacks and incredible views. Today, I'm thinking, it should also be famous for its horrible traffic. It's a beautiful road and the scenery is breath taking, but I would have liked to have been able to get out of first gear! Oh well, it is what it is. We did the road going east all the way to St. Mary's, turned around and did it going west. It's gorgeous in both directions; high mountain passes, turquoise blue lakes, tumbling round stoned rivers, fresh air scented with pine and fir and cedar. I love mountains – incredibly powerful and timeless . . . raw nature.

Day 7: July 8
Glacier National Park to
Havre, Montana

Parting is such sweet sorrow. It's hard to leave my friends . . . sometimes we drive each other crazy, but I love them to pieces. Last night at our campfire, I left for a few minutes and when I came back, there was something (someone?) in my chair.

It was a Teddy Bear all dressed up in Harley motorcycle gear – even a helmet and sunglasses. So cute! The girls got him for me and he's adorable. He sits on the back of my bike and is my new traveling companion. Now I will never be lonely because I'm not alone. He's the perfect man and such a good listener. Of course, I named him Ted . . . what else would you name a Teddy Bear?

Big hugs when the girls and I parted ways this afternoon. I'm scared, excited, happy, and sad all at the same time. I need to readjust and find my own balance now for this trip. I didn't get on the road today until two o'clock (it takes forever to pack up camping gear and say farewell to friends) but I managed to put 350 km behind me. So I decided to treat myself to a motel. Ahhh, the joys of a hot shower and a comfy bed.

DAY 8: July 9
Havre, Montana to Williston,

North Dakota

Met a nice couple in the motel parking lot as I was packing up this morning. He retired from the army a week ago and they are on their way to Alaska. They have a bright yellow Honda Gold-wing with a matching trailer named Tweetie . . . with a big stuffed Tweetie Bird on the back. When I asked him if they were camping, he pointed to the trailer and said, "No, that's my makeup bag!" LOL.

I stopped to take a break in a town called Wolf Point just because the name interested me. There was a Saturday market going on in a local park. This is Sioux country and the market was full of First Nations handicrafts. I talked with a few of the artisans as I wandered from booth to booth. One of them commented on my aboriginal earrings. "They're Haida eagles," I said. He nodded, serious and silent.

I'm trying to pace myself as I ride, I'm trying to find my balance, but the days seem so long. I decide to stay in a motel in Williston tonight.

DAY 9: July 10
Williston to Turtle River State Park, Arvilla, North Dakota

What an amazing day! Beautiful sunshine and, man, is it ever hot. Riding on the prairies, the day always begins with a hoody, leather jacket and chaps. After 100 km, I take a break and take off the hoody. After another 100 km, I stop and get something to eat and take off the chaps. After another 100 km, I take a break again and open all the vent zippers in my leather jacket. During the final 100 km, I begin figuring out where I'm going to sleep.

Today I finally started to find my balance. It felt so good. I need a routine that's flexible and works for me. Today was perfect. Keeping my speed down and taking frequent breaks lets me cover more kilometers and feel less tired.

North Dakota is more varied than eastern Montana. There's actually things to look at while you're riding – hills and trees and lakes. In eastern Montana it was so flat that I was worried that I would fall asleep with my eyes open. Not a smart thing to do when you're going highway speed.

On my first break of the day I met a guy on a Harley named Rich. We sat and talked after we gassed up. He's been to the Sturgis Harley Rally 11 times. He lives in a town in North Dakota with a population of 120 people. He said that ND has changed since the oil boom, "It's not as friendly as it used to be."

Rich told me that on long rides he takes a break every hour. For me an hour is usually 100 km. Good time to gas up, eat a little, drink water and visit the washroom. I appreciated having confirmation from Rich that my frequent breaks are a sensible routine. He asked me when we parted if I was a hugger. I said, "Yes," and he gave me a great big bear hug. Super nice.

After riding for hundreds of kilometers in beautiful sunshine on gently curving roads through gorgeous scenery, I notice on the map that there is a state park called Turtle River only 80 km away and they have camping. I check the weather on my phone and the thunderstorm forecasted for tomorrow has disappeared. Hooray! No motel tonight. I'm gonna camp.

I set up my tent, get water, build a fire, make dinner and I'm a happy little camper. I do so love sleeping outside, but I would appreciate it if someone would please tell the mosquitos to stop feasting on me!

DAY 10: July 11
Turtle River State Park to
Grand Rapids, Minnesota

Oh well, I guess I goofed when I checked my weather app yesterday – that thunderstorm didn't disappear, it came with a vengeance at 2 a.m. The thunder was so loud that it woke me up; an absolute downpour accompanied it. Torrential rain! Thank goodness I had covered up all my gear before going to bed and I was warm and dry in my cozy little tent. The rain stopped in the morning and I was able to pack up without getting wet. I rode off under grey leaden threatening skies hoping that the rain would hold off.

It was so much work packing up my wet tent that I didn't even cook breakfast; I just had yogurt and a granola bar. I stopped in a little town called Erskine about a 100 km down the road to have breakfast. The restaurant was called Ness Café and it was established in 1912. The owner, Diane, is in her early 50s and super friendly. She asked me where I was going and where I was from and admired Ted waiting patiently for me on the back of my bike. She said she thought my trip was, "pretty cool."

After I finished my breakfast, Diane asked me what I thought about the T-shirts in the window. I said I liked the tank top and did she have a size small. She got one out for me to try on and also handed be a light purple long sleeved hoody that she'd just gotten in. I tried on the hoody; it was so soft it felt like a warm hug. When I asked how much, Diane said it was a gift for me to take on my trip. It was like she was saying, "You go girl! Do it for me too!"

Leaving Erskine, the sky still threatened rain. The clouds were a low roof over my head stretching all the way around the horizon, depressing shades of grey. But I did a smart thing, smart for me anyway because sometimes I can be too stubborn: when the sky finally opened and the rain poured down, I rode it out for 100 km and then I called it quits.

It takes a lot of concentration to ride in the rain. The road is awash and there are two frothy rivulets running in the depressions made by truckers' tires. Do I ride in the grease strip between the depressions where cars have leaked oil? Or do I ride where I normally do in the left depression? I choose the grease strip; the rivulets are frothy white, which usually means they're rain mixed with oil washed from the grease strip into the depressions and super slippery.

I know my traction in these conditions is compromised; I reduce my speed and focus on keeping the rubber side down. I'm doing 10 km under the speed limit, which means cars are coming up fast behind me. I have to watch to make sure that they see me and pass me safely. I have to be aware that I may need to move to the shoulder if they do something really stupid. It's very, very, very tiring.

I call it a day after 300 km. Get a cheap motel in Grand Rapids and have Subway and beer for dinner. Lay out my wet riding gear all over the motel room to dry and put my soggy boots upside down on the heat register. Have a hot shower and cozy up in bed. Good night.

DAY 11: July 12
Grand Rapids, Minnesota
to Prentice, Wisconsin

Woke up to sunshine and a cloudless sky. Hooray! A beautiful day to ride. Stopped for gas and a snack 100 km down the road. I was standing by my bike drinking a carton of milk when a man stopped to admire Ruby. He introduced himself as David. He said he used to ride a Honda Gold Wing before his back got bad.

I asked David if his wife enjoyed riding and he replied, "My Nita passed away in April." I told him I was sorry and he responded, "We had 34 wonderful years together." Then he started to tell me about her. A couple times he interrupted himself and said, "I hope you don't mind. My Nita always said I talk too much, but talking about her is my way of healing."

David explained that Nita had been in a wheelchair for the past seven years, but that she never complained and always had a positive attitude. During the past year it became harder for her to do things for herself, so he would help her get out of bed and into her wheelchair and do whatever she needed done.

At Easter, David invited four of his wife's girlfriends over and cooked Easter dinner for them. He said he helped Nita into her wheelchair and surprised her with a dressing gown in her favorite colors that he'd had specially made for her with matching slippers and a knitted cap (because she was self-conscious that she'd lost all her hair). He wheeled his beautiful Nita into the living room just as her girlfriends arrived.

David told me that she laughed and chatted with her girl-friends and was livelier than she'd been in ages. After several hours, she said to her friends, "Y'all gotta go now cuz I'm about ready to fall out of this wheelchair!" David told me that when he lifted her out of the wheelchair and put her back into her bed, she took his hand and said, "Sit down here beside me, I got somethin' I gotta tell ya."

As he sat on the bed and held her she said softly, "David, I'm dying." He said, "I know, baby." He told me that they kissed; then he smiled to himself at the memory and said, "We even necked a bit." After that day, David said it was like a light switch went off. She died a few weeks later.

He made a wooden box with hearts interlocking on all four corners. He had his wedding band cut, intertwined with hers and soldered back together. He put their wedding bands and her fa-vorite picture of the two of them in the wooden heart box and buried it with her.

As David is telling me all this, tears are streaming down my face. I couldn't help it. He said that in all the years they were mar-ried, there was never a bad year. He explained, "I don't think there was ever a day when my Nita thought about divorcing me," he paused and smiled, "But I know that there were several occasions when she would've liked to kill me!" And he laughed.

I can't help crying as I write this. I told David I was really sorry that she was gone. But I also told him how fortunate I thought he was, "You are really lucky that you had her in your life for 34 years. Some people never get to experience the kind of love that you two shared."

Highway #2 has become my friend. I've been on this road for five days through Montana, North Dakota, Minnesota and now Wisconsin. I planned on taking Highway #2 all the way into Mich-igan. So imagine my surprise when just east of Ashland, Wisconsin

I encounter a huge barricade stretching across both lanes of the highway with the words Road Closed emblazoned on it.

There's a state trooper who explains to me and a dozen other drivers that the big storm last night washed out Highway #2 going east and several roads going south. She asks me where I was trying to get to and when I mention Marquette, Michigan she responds, "Well hon, you can't get there from here." She sends me back 100 km to a road going south that isn't washed out. That's 200 km and three hours of my day wasted.

Now to get to Marquette, it means a 550 km detour: I opt to change plans instead. Visiting Marquette will have to wait until the return trip. If I take a more southern route through Wisconsin, it adds up to a loss of 200 km instead of 550. I continue on my way in the sunshine, enjoying the forest scenery and the numerous small towns.

I stop at Cameron, Minnesota for gas and a stretch, and ask a local guy who's gassing up his truck if there are any motels within the next 100 km east of here. He says, "It's nice to see a woman rider." That's a rather strange answer. We get to talking and he queries, "I guess you're not married?" And that's a pretty upfront question, but when I respond, "No," his next question is even bolder; "So what happened?"

I reply that when I told my ex he should quit doing things that did not benifit him or us, he didn't listen. Greg (by now we'd introduced ourselves) laughs and says, "Men aren't very good at doing what they're told to!" When I agree, he adds, "But then neither are women!" At this I laugh too.

Turns out he was born and raised in Cameron and runs a second-hand business. He picks up stuff that people don't want and sells it to people who want it. Keeps him busy, so busy that regretfully he finds it hard to find time to ride his Heritage Soft Tail. Greg wishes me a "safe ride," and I keep heading east. Get a motel in the tiny town of Prentice. Very tired. Ruby and I did 600 km today, but only 400 in the right direction.

DAY 12: July 13
Prentice, Wisconsin to
Manistique, Michigan

What a terrible motel that was! Over-priced and no amenities! The only thing positive about that place was the friendly local people who worked there. The owner was an a-hole who treated his employees like crap. Note to self: don't stay in small towns with only one motel; they jack up the price because you've got nowhere else to go.

I had a good sleep but I'm tired today, probably because yesterday I did more kilometers than I usually do. The heat reflecting off the pavement is hotter than hell, and the wind is howling at me from the side. I have to brace myself against it by leaning slightly into it because it's trying to push me over into the oncoming traffic; yet every time I go past a little hill or a group of trees, the wind pressure eases and I need to lean less or I will fall right over. I suppose it's kind of funny, but it takes considerable muscle power and concentration to stay centered in my lane.

But, Yes!, I'm finally in Michigan! Riding along the northern edge of Lake Michigan, I get beautiful glimpses through the trees of waves beating against the shoreline. The wind has taken its toll on me though; I'm ready to call it a day. I stop at the info center in Manistique to ask for a motel recommendation. Connie, the woman who works there, suggests Gray Wolf Lodge. She explains that it's not the cheapest place in town, but after a hard day's ride she figures I should treat myself and enjoy the hot tub, swimming pool, and view of the lake. Is she a rider? Of course she is; she knows what your body wants at the end of the day. She certainly didn't have to twist my arm very hard. And it's way less expensive than where I stayed last night.

DAY 13: July 14

Manistique to Pinconning, Michigan

Oh what a lovely sleep. What a wonderful motel. I am very happy I stayed here last night. That hot tub did wonders for my aching, tired body.

Didn't think it was going to rain this morning so I didn't put on my raingear. That was a mistake. I got about thirty minutes down the road and had to pull over on the shoulder to suit up. Not fun, since the shoulder was narrow and the cars and trucks were whistling by. Once I got going again, I passed several bikers on the shoulder doing exactly what I'd just done. I guess the rain caught more than me by surprise.

Had brunch in St. Ignace, a very touristy little town, and then said a short prayer before heading for the mighty Mackinaw Bridge. The bridge is five miles long, connects the upper peninsula of Michigan to the lower peninsula and crosses over the straits where Lake Michigan flows into Lake Huron. There's an urban legend about a Volkswagen being blown off the bridge during a storm; I don't want to think about adding my Harley to the story. Today there's a super strong wind coming from the west across Lake Michigan and I know I will get hammered by it on the bridge. It's so windy that even the cars are crawling at a snail's pace. I survived.

I said goodbye to my old friend Highway #2 and hopped on super highway Interstate 75. It feels strange to be on a divided highway with cars going 110 to 120 km. I'm keeping my speed at 100 because that's what the speed limit is and its way less tiring for me. I appreciate that people give me lots of space when they pass me.

Stopped at Gaylord for a break and – surprise! It was their annual fair with carnival rides and games and all kinds of booths selling food and crafts. I was drawn to a booth with beautiful stone jewelry (God, I love rocks!) made by a woman named Marge. We talked for a while about all sorts of things, especially a trip she and her husband took to Victoria, B.C. a couple of years ago. Her husband, Dennis had wanted to buy a bowler hat, get out their croquet set, and play croquet on the Parliament Building lawn. No, she didn't let him.

Of course I bought a ring; it has copper brick set in it. Copper brick comes from the flues of abandoned copper mines. Its ceramic firebrick infiltrated over decades with smelted copper. It reminds me of the years I spent living in Marquette, Michigan, the port on Lake Superior where the copper was shipped out.

Cruising down Interstate 75, I was torn by indecision. Should I keep going? It's only about three more hours to my Mom's house and it's not raining and it might rain tomorrow. But I've already been on the road for eight hours. I stopped in Pinconning at a gas station and asked about a motel I had seen advertised on a billboard. A nice young girl googled it on her phone and showed me how to get there.

Instead I got lost; I must have driven right by the motel and totally missed it. I came to the end of a dead-end road and – surprise again – I'm at the gate of a rural county campground set on the beachfront of Lake Huron! Alrighty then, I'm a camper tonight. I'm going to fall asleep to the sound of the wind in the trees.

DAY 14: July 15
Pinconning to Brighton, Michigan

Had a long chat last night with Park Ranger Curtis. I learned all about fishing for Walleyes (a kind of fish), and how the waters of Saginaw Bay are full of Honeyholes (places where fish hang out). He said that 90 per cent of the people staying at Pinconning Park are here for the fishing. Well, I guess that makes me part of the 10 per cent. Since there are 50 campsites, I'm one of five people who are not here to fish. I wonder who the other four are?

Mostly Ranger Curtis talked about his wife. He told me that things haven't been going too well for the past year. He said that it seems like they're always arguing and he doesn't know how to make it better. He met her when he was 14, got married at 17 and promptly had three kids. Both he and his wife grew up in neighboring small towns. I really didn't know what to say to help him out. But maybe he didn't need me to say anything; maybe he just needed me to listen, which I did.

Our conversation made me think – what are the most important things to me in a relationship? What is my definition of the perfect Man? Well, he's kind and caring and smart and funny and honest and hardworking. Those are all attributes; what does he DO to demonstrate those attributes? It's a person's actions that communicate how much you love someone. Actions are so much louder than words. "Partnership" is how I envision a successful relationship.

Lovely to wake up to the sound of birds and it didn't even take me that long to pack up my camping gear and load Ruby. Cloudy day, but it doesn't look like rain. I'm heading for the Harley Davidson dealer in Brighton. I'm going to have them check out Ruby's clutch while I visit with my Mom over the weekend. I'm really looking forward to spending time with her. I love her so much.

Gee whiz, I am good at getting lost. Eventually, I always find my way, but why do I have to go through the lost part so often? Interstate 75 and Highway #23 were full of traffic, road construction, and people in a hurry; it was absolute insanity. I missed the exit for Brighton and ended up almost in Anne Arbor. Frustrating; I had to stop and ask for directions twice.

I had phoned the Brighton Harley shop a couple days earlier from Manistique to let them know I was having clutch trouble and asked if they had time on Friday to check out my bike. Ozzie, the service manager, said they had an opening at 2:30. I hesitated and said I wasn't sure if I could make it by then. Ozzie got kind of owly and snapped, "You said you'd be here on Friday. Do you want the 2:30 spot or not?"

I wanted to ask him who had pissed in his corn flakes this morning, but instead I replied, "I'm a 63-year-old woman traveling from the west coast by myself. Right now I'm in Wisconsin and it's raining. I'm not even in Michigan yet. I know I can make it to Brighton by Friday, but I don't know if I can get there by 2:30." Ozzie softened up a bit, "Can you make it here before closing on

Friday and we'll look at your bike on Saturday?" I said, "Yes."

I arrived at the shop Friday afternoon and went to the service department. I figure its Ozzie sitting behind the counter talking to a customer. He looks up at me, "Mary, Mary, quite contrary," he says slowly. "That would be me," I reply smiling.

When Ozzie finishes with the other customer, he talks to me. Unfortunately, the mechanic won't be able to look at Ruby until Sunday. "But I want to be back on the road by Monday and what if you need to order parts?" I ask imploringly. "It's highly unlikely that we won't have the parts," he remarks.

Ozzie hops on my bike to ride it into the shop. He shifts her into first gear and then his eyes go wide as Ruby takes off at 20 km – with the clutch all the way in. I laugh. I've been dealing with this for 3,000 km. Ozzie has the mechanic look at my bike right away. He makes it clear to me that it's "for diagnoses only right now."

While I'm waiting for my Mom to come pick me up, the mechanic comes out to talk to me. "Holy shit!" he exclaims. "I started your bike up and she drove herself right into my workbench!"

"You didn't hurt her, I hope?" I ask. "No, he says, "But you need a whole new clutch and we don't have the parts. We'll have to order them in and it'll take four or five days." I look straight at Ozzie and slowly repeat his words, "It's highly unlikely that we won't have the parts."

"I'll phone a couple of dealers," he says quickly. "Maybe one of them will have your clutch in stock."

Meanwhile, my Mom arrives. She starts talking with one of the Harley salesmen while I am busy with Ozzie and the mechanic. When I finish making arrangements for Ruby's repair, my Mom and I exchange big hugs and she introduces me to the sales guy. It turns out that my Mom has been telling him all about my trip and how worried she is about me. (Sounds just like a classic mom, doesn't she?) The salesman says to her with a motorcyclist's enthusiasm, "You should be really proud of your daughter. Riding across the country is an amazing adventure!" My Mom laughs and agrees. We both know I inherited my adventurous spirit from her.

Ozzie turns out to be a mechanical magician. He phones me a

couple hours later and says my bike is fixed. He found the clutch parts, made fixing my bike a priority and it's done. To say I thanked him profusely would be an understatement.

Ozzie is a really good guy. He served in the Vietnam War, was a prison guard for 30 years, and then worked with youth-at-risk in high schools. We talked about some of the teenagers he worked with. It's obvious he has a soft spot in his heart for them still. He's got an off-the-cuff sense of humor, but what strikes me most about him are his eyes. He looks right at you when you're talking with him, like he's really listening and absorbing every word. I bet that's what made him so good at working with the so-called bad boys.

DAY 15: July 16
Mom's House, Brighton, Michigan

It's such a wonderful feeling to be with my Mom at home. I bet almost everybody in the whole world feels that way about their mom . . . moms are special. But my Mom is extra special. She raised us three kids on her own, worked a full-time job, and always made sure she was there for us. That's what I remember the most: anytime I needed my Mom, she was there for me. And today, like always, she's thinking of my sister and brother and me; I don't manage to see them as often as I'd like, so my Mom has arranged for me to spend all day today with my brother, John, and tomorrow with my sister, Nancy.

I just have to say that my brother John is, without a doubt, the best brother in the entire world! He's smart and funny, kind and thoughtful, and a great dad to his kids. He took me for a cruise on the lake in his speedboat for the whole afternoon and we drank beer and laughed about all sorts of memories from our childhood:

How he egged our hateful neighbor's house several times because she made us get rid of our beloved dog, Queenie.

How much fun he had going to dog shows with our Dad; he got to do whatever he wanted while I had to work my buns off grooming dogs.

How he got lost at the amusement park and hardly got to go on any rides, while I went on all of them.

How on summer family camping adventures, fishing and boating were the best! We'd constantly get our fishing line snagged on the bottom of the lake and have to cut the lines and put on new hooks. We caught tons of tiny perch that Mom had to try to fillet until she instituted a catch-and-release policy.

How I always used to see him out in the hall at school (kicked out of class again), but I never told Mom because I didn't want him to get into more trouble.

How I was so bummed out when my bike got stolen, but then John found it, angrily confronted the guy and got it back for me.

How I taught him to swim by taking him out into the lake over his head and then letting him go.

I asked John how he managed to become such a great dad – because he really is wonderful with his kids – when he had such a poor role model. He said it's because he wanted his kids to have everything that he didn't have. Well, he succeeded. I love my brother!

DAY 16: July 17
Mom's House, Brighton, Michigan

And I also have the best sister in the entire world. She is such a hard worker, always thinking about and taking care of people, upbeat, happy, and able to see the positive side in any situation. I know it drives her crazy that I am kind of flying by the seat of my pants on this trip, and it makes her worry about me.

So Nancy spent hours on the computer this afternoon, googling maps and checking out campgrounds, while I sat beside her and took copious notes. She set me up with a plan of action for the next five days which bypasses major cities (thank God), allows me to ride as much as possible on secondary highways instead of expressways, keeps me under 400 km per day, puts me in a four-star campground every night, and gets me to Fredericton, New Brunswick in time for my daughter Kat's music festival. Hooray!

We also planned a trip to Yellowstone National Park with my Mom for next year in July. A lot of the reservations for a national park need to be made a full year in advance; thank goodness my sister is so organized.

I really, really, admire her – Nancy has had to pick herself up by the bootstraps and recreate her life several times. During the recession, she lost her high paying executive position with a big insurance company. She put out tons of applications for work with no responses. She finally found a job selling franchises; sales was not something she had ever done before. But she's very successful at it and her clients love her because she's willing to go the distance to support them. On top of that, she has raised two wonderful children. My sister is an amazing woman and I love her to pieces.

DAY 17: July 18
Brighton, Michigan to Milton, Ontario

My sister is so very thoughtful. She slept over at Mom's again last night and let work know she was coming in late so she could escort me through the confusing "circles of death," otherwise known as traffic circles, and get me headed in the right direction on the highway. Thank you, Nancy!

Boy, these roads are different than my old friend Highway #2 across the prairies. Everyone is going a million miles an hour and there's lots of construction and lane closures. Crossed the border over the Blue Water Bridge between Port Huron, Michigan and Sarnia, Ontario. The line-up was long and I had to keep putting Ruby into neutral. Love the new clutch, but it's really stiff – it's hard to hold it in at a long traffic light or in a line-up. At least Ruby has neutral now.

The traffic in Ontario is the same as Lower Michigan – it must be an eastern thing. The speed limit is 100 km, I'm doing 110 km and everyone is passing me! I hope I get used to it because it will probably be like this for at least two more days.

Arrive at the wonderful campground my sister found for me. It's full of Winnebagos, but there's a nice area for tents. As soon as I pull into my site, Fernando comes over and introduces himself and his wife Anne. From the porch of his motorhome, he had seen that I was concerned about my kickstand sinking into the soft ground and he came over with a piece of wood to put under it. How kind! He says, "After you get yourself settled, come over and try some of my homemade Portuguese wine."

While I'm setting up, Jennifer in the tent site next to me pops by offering to help, and we end up chatting about motorcycles. Her father has a Honda Gold Wing, but he's getting older and it's getting too heavy for him. He had a nasty "stop and drop" with his wife on the back and they are both still healing. Jennifer texts her Dad to tell him about the girl camping next door and within minutes, he and I are Facebook friends.

After I get my tent all set up and have a bite to eat, I walk over to visit Fernando and Anne. What a lovely couple. He grew up in the Azores and came to Canada when he was nine. He describes how beautiful the islands are, (his island is a UNESCO World Heritage Site), bullfighting in Portugal (but they don't kill the bull like the Spanish do), running with the bulls in the street (bulls run faster than people, so you always have to keep your eyes out for a wall or tree to climb), and how gorgeous the beaches and ocean are. He's very handsome and just crazy enough to be appealing.

I can see why Anne married him. She's about the same age as me and Fernando is her second husband. She's warm and loving, and definitely runs the relationship. It's obvious that Fernando adores her. They lived in B.C. for several years so we compare thoughts about the Okanagan Valley, Whistler and North Vancouver. During the past three years they've been retired and traveling in their motorhome. They spend six months a year in Canada and six months a year in the southern US. Nice lifestyle. They are both very relaxed and happy. And Fernando's homemade Portuguese wine is delicious.

While I was riding the highway today, I saw a billboard that said, *The Power of the Journey.* I couldn't read the rest, the print was too small, but I don't think it matters. It made me think – yes, this journey is very powerful to me. I don't really know what I'm here to learn or how all these amazing people and incredible experiences fit together. It's like a picture puzzle and you only have one piece in your hand at a time and you don't know what the puzzle will look like when it's completed, but you do know that someway somehow all the pieces are meant to fit together.

DAY 18: July 19
Milton to Johnstown, Ontario

Oh man! I'm moving like a herd of turtles this morning. Made myself some oatmeal and coffee, enjoyed the peacefulness, and wrote in my journal. Didn't hit the road until noon. Maybe I was procrastinating because I'm not looking forward to being on the #401 again with all those crazy people going a million miles an hour.

A truck driver in the campground came over to chat with me. He gave me a tip when I complained about nut-bar drivers, "Ride in the right-hand lane with the trucks," he advised. "They'll give you space and they drive like you ride – they watch ahead and slow down if something is happening. They don't want to come to a stop 'cuz it takes too much to get the rig moving again, so they anticipate the changes in traffic flow to always keep the wheels rolling."

I tried riding in the right-hand lane, even though I am a little scared being among the trucks; they are huge. But they drive more sanely than the people in cars. It doesn't take me long to figure out that the truckers also know when the right-hand lane is going to turn into "Exit Only" and they move over. I followed one semi for more than an hour. He was doing 105 kmph; my favorite speed for long distances. He got me all the way through Toronto, which is a veritable maze of incomprehensible interchanges. Before I exited to take a break and gas up, I passed him and gave him a big wave. I knew that he knew I was back there the whole time.

But hitting the road at noon does not give me time to stop and see things along the way. I can only do one-stop-shopping – gas up, eat something, drink water, pee, stretch, and get back on the road. Gas stations along the expressway are not very scenic; convenient but they have nil for ambience.

By the time I was able to get off the #401 and take a secondary highway east, it was late in the afternoon. I was passing through beautiful little towns, yet I knew if I stopped, I would be driving after dark. That's an absolute no-no for me – drunks and deer are too big of a hazard. When I pass this way again on my return trip west, I promise myself that I will stop at some of them, especially Gananoque. It's old fashioned and the "painted ladies" are the most gorgeous I have ever seen. Funky little stores on Main Street, bakeries and wonderful weird clothing and antique shops.

I'm riding and riding and it's getting later and later and I'm wondering if I should just grab a motel instead of continuing to the campground Nancy and I picked out. Suddenly the road starts to wind along right next to the St. Lawrence Seaway and the Thousand Islands come into view. Across the river, the full moon begins to rise in the east as the sun is setting in the west and the whole sky is a kaleidoscope of soft pinks and purples and blues. Beyond amazing!

Minutes later, there's a sign for my campground. My campsite is right on the St. Lawrence and the woman who owns the place says to me, "Half price for motorcyclists." Is she a rider? Of course she is. She has a red Honda Shadow.

Set-up my tent just before dark. I heat up some dinner and sit on my picnic table watching the moon rise higher and higher in the sky. It's so bright I can see my shadow. It's quieter than quiet; I can hear the fish jumping. It's a good day/night to be alive.

DAY 19: July 20
Johnstown, Ontario to Levis, Quebec

Beautiful morning! Woke up early and decided to have a shower, it's been a few days . . . felt so good. Another slow start to the day. I got up at sunrise and that gives me the right to move at a turtle's pace, doesn't it?

Chatted for a long time with a camping neighbor, Danielle. She has a trailer that she and her husband are staying in. At least I thought it was her husband, but it turns out that he's her boyfriend. She said they've been together for a year. Her passion in life is ice fishing! She's got her own truck, a gas auger (to drill the hole) and a fishing shanty that she drags behind the truck across the ice. Wow, that sounds cool! It's not something I have ever experienced. I think we really admired the strength in each other. Very, very neat lady! Big hugs when we parted.

I like small towns; the secondary highways go straight through them and they have interesting things to see. In medium sized towns, the secondary highways snake through them, there's no signage and I inevitably get lost. I think that's what they want you to do – then you have to stop to ask directions, so you get something to eat or shop. And big cities; well, it's best if I just go around them. That in itself is stressful.

I had to go around Montreal today. Thankfully, I met a Quebecois woman rider at a gas station with her girlfriend on the back. She confirmed the route Nancy had googled for me. Yes! But for some reason, I'm feeling really tired late in the day. Maybe it's the stress of the expressway and all the traffic around Montreal, even though I hit it at midday to avoid morning and evening rush hour.

At the end of the day, when I was only a few miles from my next camping spot, I dropped my bike. (Mom, if you are reading this, I'm fine, I didn't hurt myself. And I want you to know that there are only two types of riders in the world – those that admit they've dropped their bike and those that are lying!)

It was a busy intersection with no traffic light. Heavy traffic coming from both directions, poor visibility because of a bridge, and I'm trying to make a left on an upward slope. Someone had taken a spray can and painted "Danger" across my left-hand turn lane. They were right. So being the cautious careful person I am, I sat there and waited for an opening in the traffic. I must have been there for 10 minutes. Usually when I have to sit and wait for that long of a time, I shift into neutral because my lovely brand-new clutch is stiff. But I didn't; I wanted to be ready when the opening appeared.

Finally the guy coming from my left stopped and then the guy coming from my right stopped and waved for me to go. They were aware that it's a tough intersection to make a left turn and were giving me a break. I guess my fingers were stiff from holding the clutch so long and I didn't feather it right. Anyway, I powered out and stalled. When you stall with the wheel turned on an uphill, there can be only one result – you and the bike go down.

Thankfully I didn't try to hold Ruby up . . . I let her go. It was a slow-motion fall and I didn't hurt my beautiful bike or myself – just shattered my confidence in front of an audience of about thirty cars.

The guys who had stopped on my right and left, and the guy behind me, immediately put on their four way flashers and jumped out of their vehicles. They only spoke French, but they were obviously asking if I was OK. I nodded and picked myself up off the pavement. They righted my bike – between the three of them they made it look like it took no effort at all and waited while I got back on. They hopped back in their trucks and continued to hold all the traffic back while I took a deep breath, started the engine and made my left-hand turn.

I'm thankful that my instinctive reaction was not to try to keep Ruby upright; the last time I did that I broke my arm. I'm thankful that those gallant knights in shining armor leaped out of their vehicles, helped me get the rubber side of Ruby back where it belonged on the pavement and held back traffic until I got going again.

But what could I have done differently so that the whole situation didn't occur? I should have recognized that the intersection was a difficult place to make a left. Duh! "Danger" was written right on the pavement – that should have been my first clue! Instead of trying to turn left, I could have turned right, found a place that was safe to turn around, and then I would have been able to ride straight through that difficult intersection.

OK, lesson learned. Use your brain next time Mary Jane. A big thank you to God for keeping me from getting hurt and providing me with rescuers. Avoiding dangerous situations would be a way better plan for the future, rather than having to deal with them.

DAY 20: July 21
Levis, Quebec to Grand
Falls, New Brunswick

Now that was not my style of campground last night. There were tons of kids (and I like kids), but they were riding their bicycles all over the road (and some of them obviously just learning to ride). They had no awareness that they had to share the road with motor vehicles. I was totally paranoid I was going to have to slam on my brakes in the gravel to avoid hitting them! Jeez Louise! And on top of that, it cost me big bucks for the pleasure of staying there.

I think I'm just tired of dealing with traffic. Both Montreal and Toronto were nightmares and it's not just near the cities – the traffic stretches for 100 km in all directions. And dropping my bike yesterday didn't exactly lower my anxiety level. But today is a new day and things will be better. Leaving Levis Quebec, everything improves immediately. The highway is less busy and the scenery is gorgeous rolling hills, farms and forest. Ahhh, I can relax now!

I rode behind a trucker for about 100 km. He was doing 10 km over the speed limit, which is just right for me. He sits higher than I do and he can see things farther ahead. I made sure he could see me clearly in his rear-view mirror. A traffic situation that irritates me is when a semi puts on his blinker to move over a lane and cars keep passing; they refuse to let him in. After a while I started playing tail gunner for the trucker in front of me. He'd turn on his signal, then I'd move over safely and block the lane. He'd move over, we'd pass the slow-moving vehicle, then we'd move back into the right-hand lane again. After an hour of this I needed to get gas, so I passed him, gave him a big wave and he honked his air horn as I rode down the exit ramp. I felt like I'd made a new friend.

I got back on the road for a while, when it started to rain a bit. Took an exit so I could put on my raingear. Parked in front of a store that I thought sold groceries (the sign was in French, I'm in Quebec after all) and it turned out to be a hardware store. Well, at least they had coffee and a bathroom.

By now it had started to really pour. I sat down in a sturdy plastic rocking chair the hardware store had for sale in an out-side covered area, drank my coffee and made some phone calls to reserve a camping spot for a couple hundred km down the road. Nice way to sit out a passing shower.

The countryside became more and more beautiful as I rode into New Brunswick. Forests, lakes, big rocky cliffs – a new view around every curve. I could ride on these kinds of roads with this kind of scenery for hours without getting tired.

Arrived in Grand Falls. Guess what? They have a big waterfall here. Duh! My campground is only a couple blocks from their quaint little downtown and right on the edge of a cliff overlook-ing the river. Hooray! This is my kind of place. As usual I got lost and couldn't find the campground, but I asked a local guy on his scooter and he kindly led me there.

I met a really interesting East Indian couple from B.C. as I was checking in. At first I thought she was way too chatty; she kind of drove me crazy because she had a strong accent and I had to concentrate super hard to understand her. But her enthusiasm for life and camping and nature and seeing the big beautiful country she'd just immigrated to was infectious. Joyful is the best way to describe her.

She told me she was a Buddhist and that in the Punjabi region of India where she grew up, Buddhism is a 2,500-year-old trad-ition. She explained that the dominant religion is Sikhism and was founded about 500 years ago. Her face and her smiling expression reminded me of statues of the laughing Buddha. She had an effervescent personality and her husband was friendly too, but far quieter.

I have wonderful neighbors in this campground (once again). Jim and Elspeth are in a big camper just a couple sites down. They're both from Nova Scotia; she grew up in Cape Breton. He's wiry and thin, bald with a grizzled beard, and seems hard at first. She's pretty and blond, warm with a soft voice. They used to tour on a Honda Gold Wing until he just couldn't hold up the weight at a stop sign anymore. They traded their bike in for a camper and now they tour in comfort.

We sat and talked for a long time, about bikes and roads and truckers. I told them some of my experiences. "People are basically nice, aren't they?" asked Elspeth, kind of a question and kind of a statement at the same time. "Yes," I said, "They sort of just seem to be waiting for an opportunity to help. And when you ask them because you really need their help and then thank them afterward, they glow." You certainly wouldn't get that impression of the human race by watching the news.

DAY 21: July 22
Grand Falls to the Future Forest Festival in Zealand, New Brunswick

"Did your feathers get wet last night?" Elspeth asked me kindly this morning over coffee. No, I was cozy in my little tent listening to the raindrops on the roof...

I left Grand Falls, rode for about an hour, and decided to stop in Hartland for a coffee. Do you know that Hartland has the world's longest covered bridge? It's made out of huge timbers and is over 100 years old. Did I ride Ruby across it? Of course I did! Both ways! I had the biggest shit-eating grin on my face that you can ever imagine. It was so dark inside with just one skinny lane and huge beautiful beams. Imagine being in a horse and carriage or a Model T Ford. Wow!

Before leaving Hartland, I decided that it would be wise to ask for directions. I know that the Future Forest Festival is happening outside of Fredericton somewhere near Zealand, but I'm really not quite sure where. I asked a super friendly lady at the info center where Wark's Wilderness Getaway was. That's where the Future Forest Festival is being held. We googled it, looked at a map, and I wrote down the directions.

I have to go east from Hartland on a secondary road to get to another road that runs north/south. I ride off on this road, following the directions of the info center lady to go left, then right then left each time the road divides. I'm laughing as I ride along and name it the "Polka Dot Road." There's a pavement patch every couple feet somewhere on the road. It looks hilarious! The road is light grey (old asphalt) and the patches are dark black (new asphalt). It's like a strip of polka dot cloth running through the forest with a few dwellings on the side here and there.

Then the patches end ... and it's all potholes. Shit! I have to try to weave in and out of them. I hit one dead on and bottom out my front suspension. Ouch! I wonder if I've damaged the bike or my tire, but I keep going. The speed limit is signed at 80 km. Are you kidding me? I can only manage 50 or 60 safely. I ride on for an hour never getting out of second gear and often downshifting into first. Every time a local drives up behind me, I wait for a straight stretch, slow down, pull into the right half of my lane, and wave them past. They're happier and I'm happier. I don't want them impatiently riding my ass.

I get to the north/south road and head south. Finally – good pavement. Hooray! The info lady had said there was a gas station 10 minutes down this road; there it is ... and it's closed. I still have a third of a tank of gas left, but I don't know where there's another gas station or where the turn off for the festival is. I pull over on the side of the road to look at a map. A guy stops in a pick-up to see if I'm OK. "I'm lost and low on gas," I say. He laughs and gives me directions to the nearest gas station. It's not far.

I gas up, get directions to the festival and promptly get lost again! I know I'm on the right road – I can hear the music – but I can't find a sign. I stop and pull out the map again. A big guy with an even bigger smile comes walking down his long driveway. He's obviously heading toward me. "How did you know I needed help?" I ask him. "Well, you're parked on the side of the road looking at a map . . . it's not rocket science."

Garth invites me into his yard and introduces me to his wife and three kids. His wife rides a Harley Soft Tail and he rides a Road King. His kids are great, I chat with them (two boys and a girl) while his wife phones Wark's Wilderness Getaway to get directions. Kathy, Garth's wife, offers to have him escort me to the turnoff. I protest – they're busy and they have three little kids and she's in the middle of trying to make dinner. "He'd love to go for a ride," she says smiling.

Garth leads me down the road to the Festival turnoff. I didn't see the sign for Wark's Wilderness Getaway because there isn't one heading south – there's only one if you're heading north. Go figure! I say goodbye to Garth and look at the gravel road I'm about to ride on. He looks at me like I'm crazy to even think about taking my bike up this road, but he doesn't say so, just wishes me a "safe ride and hope the rain holds off." It's starting to thunder and lightning already.

I take a big breath and start up the road. It's obviously well used, full of ruts, more potholes, and loose gravel. I remind myself not to even think about touching the front brake. I'm hoping the Future Forest Festival is a short distance away; turns out it's not – it's five km to the main gate. I push down on my foot pegs to lower my center of gravity, keep my speed up, but not too fast, and try to pick my way around the worst of the ruts, potholes and loose gravel.

The road divides . . . shit! I go up the wrong one and realize it after a few yards. But there's no room to turn around and I can't get good enough footing to back up. A pick-up truck stops. (Thanks Universe for sending people to help me . . . continually!)

A guy gets out and asks, "Do you need help?" I respond, "YES!" and explain to him how to straddle my front wheel, and push on my front forks gently. He's perfectly steady and gets me backed up enough that I can turn onto the road I'm supposed to be on. I say thanks and, "I'm slow – you go ahead of me." A girl inside the truck calls out, "Nope. We're going to stay behind you in case you need help again." The guy laughs, agrees, and gets back in the truck.

I keep going down the road and the young couple in the truck give me lots of space and stay a good distance behind. I concentrate on keeping Ruby shiny side up, going slow but not too slow, keeping the revs up and feathering the clutch while chunks of gravel are pinging against her underside.

Finally, I arrive at the main gate. Lightning flashes across the sky and the first drops of rain begin to fall. I tell the guy at the gate Kat's name and that she is a performer and that my name is on his list for a pass. But my name is not on his list! I'm starting to get a little anxious because once the rain hits, this road is going to be as slippery as snot. A girl overhears me mention Kat's name. She exclaims, "Oh, you're Kat's Mom!" and gives me a big hug, introduces herself as Shannon and talks the gatekeeper into giving me a wristband.

OK . . . I'm in. Now I just have to figure out where to park and where to camp. And the rain hits. It's not too bad, not a downpour anyway, but I'm getting wet. Same rutty, pot holey, gravely road . . . but now with cars parked chock-a-block on both sides and people walking down the middle. Pulling in the clutch and revving the engine gets them to move over more effectively than the horn. I need some space to keep my balance and pick my way along this road.

I find a place to park and a friendly guy helps me back in to it. Another guy comes over and says I can't park there. The first guy helps me move. The second guy comes back again and says I can't park there either. Gee whiz! I thank the first guy for all his help and decide to go back up the road to where there was a sign for the TeaHive. I know that Kat is part of that group and maybe I can find a place to park near there, although I didn't see any parking when

I went past the first time.

And Lo and Behold . . . right in front of the TeaHive is a parking spot and its level! I pull Ruby in and gratefully put the kickstand down. I am not going to move her. We have been on the road for three weeks and now we are going to spend four whole days and three nights in the same place. Yes!

The TeaHive is abuzz with people and I tell the lovely lady serving tea that I'm Kat's Mom and I'm wondering if Kat is around. Big warm enthusiastic hugs, "She told us you were coming!"

"I'm so happy to meet you!"

"It's so cool you came this far to see her perform!"

I must have happily hugged and been introduced to 10 people in as many minutes. When I ask for a suggestion as to where to set up my tent, one of the girls replies, "Oh, come camp in the back with us!" and leads me behind the TeaHive where there are already lots of tents set up but plenty of room for one more. "Oh yeah," she says, "and that's Kat's car right next to you. I'm sure she'll be around in a while!"

How did I end up in exactly the right place after so many wrong turns? I really don't know, but I'm thinking life is pretty amazing.

PART II: THE MARITIMES

Map 2: The Maritimes

#19. Zealand NB: Day 22-24
#20. Oromocto NB: Day 25
#21. Fundy National Park NB: Day 26-27
#22. VictoriaVale NS: Day 28-30
#23. Blomidon Provincial Park NS: Day 31
#24. Halifax NS: Day 32-33
#25. Battery Provincial Park NS: Day 34
#26. Highlands National Park Ingonish NS: Day 35-36
#27. Highlands National Park Cheticamp NS: Day 37
#28. Wreck Cove NS: Day 38
#29. Halifax NS: Day 39-41
#30. Ovens Natural Park Riverport NS: Day 42-44
#31. Yarmouth NS: Day 45

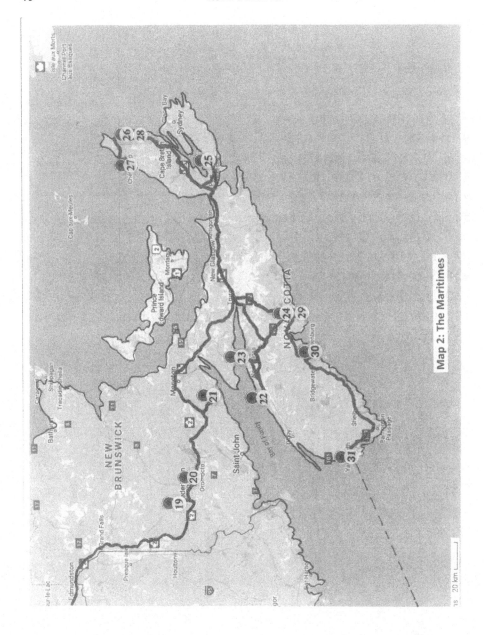

Map 2: The Maritimes

DAY 22, 23, 24: July 23, 24, 25
Future Forest Festival in
Zealand, New Brunswick

I don't know how to begin describing this place, this space, this event, this vibe; all I can do is start writing and hope that something coherent will evolve.

In the process of setting up my tent, at least twenty people come by to give me hugs and welcome me. Finally I get to meet Kat's friends in person; people she's told me about the past couple years; warm, beautiful people.

And then Kat appears – she's stoked, high energy, big hugs, laughing, and more big hugs. She explains that she has several jobs at this festival. She's stage-managing the Magic Mushroom Stage with her boyfriend, Shawn, working in the TeaHive which is a community-gathering place and harm reduction center, performing her electronic music as Nausikaa, and performing as a fire dancer with Industribe. She shows me a schedule of when she is on stage and points out some other acts that I might enjoy. And then she bounces off...

I spend the evening wandering around, checking out where things are and meeting more people. There are three stages, all a bit of a distance from each other so the music doesn't overlap. Just across from the TeaHive is the Mushroom Stage. Enormous eight feet tall mushrooms constructed of wire and cloth surround the stage and dance area. Stairs lead to large wooden platforms perched amongst the trees, providing a bird's eye view of the performance. It's all kind of tucked in the forest and lit up with an ever-changing light show of neon colors reflecting off the huge mushrooms and the stage. Kaleidoscopic!

People say "Hi" and stop to chat. When they ask where I'm from, I say Vancouver and when they ask if I came out here just for the festival, I answer that my daughter is performing in it and that she works at the TeaHive. Immediately they exclaim, "You're

Kat's Mom!" and the hugging begins in earnest.

"She's so Beautiful."

"She's done so much for the TeaHive!"

"She's such a caring soul."

"You must be so proud of her!"

"Her music is awesome!"

"It's so cool you came all this way to see her perform."

"You created a beautiful human being."

"No, I just birthed her," I reply. "She has created her own Self."
It seems like everyone I meet knows and loves Kat. It's a beautiful
thing for a Mother's soul.

As I wander around I find two more stages; the Prism Stage is
very angular, like a prism, and is surrounded by huge whiter than
white birch trees. The music is a bit loud and harsh for my taste,
but that's probably because this stage has a large clear area in
front for dancing and partying. This is a major Party Hardy Zone!

The Vendor's Village is right next to the Prism Stage and
has hand crafted clothing, jewelry, glasswork, leatherwork and
yummy organic food. I love wandering and munching my way
through this area and checking out all the art installations that
people are in the process of creating.

The third stage is called The Nest. It is definitely my favorite
space of all. The front of the stage is covered with a magnificent
owl's face softly air brushed on flowing fabric thirty feet long
and twenty feet high. An opening in the center just below the
beak allows you to see the musicians. On the sides and above the
dance area are more air brushed fabrics which look like wings
and feathers; they're painted in the same soft blues and greens as
the owl's face. It's like being in a tent, but the sides aren't solid;
they're made of hanging feather shaped pieces of cloth that float
and drift in the slightest breeze. You feel as if you are inside and
outside at the same time. It's a very safe, welcoming space. And
the music is more low key – not as fast or pounding as the Prism
Stage. AND a sandy beach and a swimmable lake are just a few
steps behind the Nest Stage. You can listen to music, go for a
swim, attend a workshop and then listen to more music, without

really going anywhere. Love It!

I met so many of Kat's friends that I can't possibly describe each of them, but there were several who are unforgettable to me:

Nika is part of the TeaHive, as are most of Kat's friends, and she's a teacher in Halifax. We had good conversations about how much our students teach us. (Is that a strange thing for a teacher to say? But it's true!) Her curly red black hair and the way she always sits cross legged on the ground leaning up against a tree makes me imagine her as an elf.

Coco is like a big warm hug – she emanates that persona even when she's not actually hugging you! She was the first person to greet me when I went into the TeaHive; and when I said I was looking for a place to put my tent, she replied enthusiastically, "You can camp with us - we're just out the back." Big smile, warm and giving, Mother Earth, she makes you feel loved.

If Nika is an elf, and Coco is Mother Earth, then Nat is a tiny mischievous fairy! She is hilariously funny and likes to just flow whichever way the wind blows. We talked about commitment: to causes, "Yes:" to a lifelong partner, "No." She is super independent and free spirited. Nat and Kat – what a pair they are together!

And then there's Shawn, Kat's boyfriend. He reminds me of a cross between an ever-ready Energizer bunny and a Hobbit. I have the opportunity to see him in his element here at this festival. Being in charge of the Mushroom Stage is a huge job: performers, light show, and sound system, all have to be perfectly coordinated. He has a team working with him, including Kat, but the bottom line is that he is responsible for making sure that everything goes smoothly. And he takes that responsibility super seriously; he gives it all he's got and then he gives more. On top of that he has his own performances to do, both as a musician and a fire dancer. He really is like the Energizer bunny!

I meet Greg, Omri, Mariah, Blair, John, Carlton and . . . a veritable ton of Kat's friends. So many I can't remember all their names, just their warm smiles and heart-felt hugs.

It's amazing to me what Kat and her friends have put together. Everywhere you go at the festival, as soon as you mention the

TeaHive, accolades for it are profuse:
  "That place saved my life last night!"
  "The TeaHivers are so amazing!"
  "They work so hard to keep all of us safe."
  "They are such beautiful people."
  "They give and give and then give more."
The whole festival community, (participants, organizers, performers) holds the TeaHive Collective in high esteem.

What exactly is the TeaHive Collective? In Kat's words, their mandate in a nutshell is "to create a community of caring." They provide a safe space when you're too high, information about various drugs, someone to talk to if you're lost or upset, food, tea, and a quiet place to connect with others and just hang out. They have a geodesic dome frame that they set up and cover with tarps on the outside (to make it waterproof), and they cover the inside with big beautiful India print saris (to create a calm ambient atmosphere).

An excerpt from their booklet: "The TeaHive is about more than tea and space. It is a few simple but radical ideas put into practice. We are not just a space for folks having rough psychedelic experiences, but a community coming together to show the possibilities when we care for each other. It is about creating and cultivating care and constructing space and culture where true care is valued, sought and shared."

The first afternoon I was at the festival I watched Kat perform as Nausikaa. I'd heard her music before but just on the computer – not live. I must admit that I don't really understand electronic music. I'm used to watching a band with guitars, fiddles, drums, not seeing one person on stage with tons of electronic soundboards in front of them.

Kat was amazing. She performed at the Nest, my favourite stage. She chatted a bit with the audience first; welcoming them and telling them a bit about herself. Then she started; it was soft at first and then slowly gained complexity and momentum. I closed my eyes and immersed myself in her music. When I opened my eyes, I realized that the audience had grown tenfold – her music had drawn people in. Two of her friends from Industribe were in front of the stage dressed in black flowing costumes. They had choreographed a dance with long white scarves, flowing in and out, weaving the scarves and their bodies with Kat's music. Incredibly beautiful! Supported by friends, with an appreciative audience, Kat rocked it!

And then at night, I watched Kat perform with Industribe. It was at the Nest stage again, this time in total darkness except for the flames of Kat's troupe spinning and dancing and weaving with fire.

The synergy between them is amazing – sometimes they dance together – sometimes they dance alone - but the connection is always there. When one of them is performing solo, there is always an almost sacred moment as one person finishes, then passes on the flame to the next performer's torches.

Kat's troupe is very intense when they are performing. You can see it in their faces; the concentration is almost palpable. The power they emanate as they dance with fire is incredible to behold. My baby daughter is a strong beautiful woman who plays with fire. The shy girl with the big heart, who hated being the center of attention, has discovered her inner self. The beauty of that is impossible to describe . . .

DAY 25: July 26
Future Forest Festival in
Zealand To Oromocto, N.B.

There's a thing about festivals . . . it's all groovy and wonderful and loving and warm and huggy . . . and you think, "Couldn't we just live like this all the time?"

Well you can, and you can't. You can take this feeling and hold it in your heart and try to spread this love and caring in your day-to-day life in the real world. It's all about inner joy and sharing that joy with other people. When a pilgrim asked the Buddha, "What is my purpose in life?" the Buddha responded with laughter. "To be Happy!" was his reply.

But even at the festival, shit happens. We're all human beings and we bring our kaleidoscope of emotions into every environment. Someone's pissed off because someone else didn't do their job and now an overload of work is falling on too few people. Partners have spats and vocally express their frustrations. Someone is sad and feels like they should be happy but they just can't get there. "It is what it is . . ." says Kat.

"Darkness is part of life and not something to hide. It would be limiting to our lives to only be awake during the day and never explore the night, just as it is to hate and hide our sadness. It's in the dark places that we often find openings to overcome our long held fears and grow inwardly." (from the TeaHive Collective.)

I was hanging out this morning talking with Ryan and Blair and Ollie and Kendra and Kat and Shawn. They are the skeleton crew. Out of 1,500 people, there are maybe 50 to 75 still here; taking stages down, putting things into over packed cars and cleaning up. Movement is in slow-motion: Everyone is tired, but it's a happy tiredness – the festival went well and it's so good to see old friends, meet new ones and work together on a common vision. Thank you for sharing this experience with me.

I finally get on the road about 3:00. I guess I'm moving in slow motion too! Ride the five km of gravel road out; it's more packed down now after the rain and having so many cars pounding it flat. Wouldn't say it was a piece of cake, but definitely way easier than coming in.

I'm heading for Fundy National Park; I know I won't get there today but I want to at least make it part way. The sun is getting low in the sky and that thought that always occurs at this time of day comes up: "I should get more miles done before it gets dark!"

I push the thought of doing more mileage away. Instead I'm going to book into a little motel I just passed. I turn around, check in, have a shower, do my laundry (out of necessity - I'm wearing my last pair of clean underwear), order a vegie pizza and chat with Christina, the motel receptionist. She has 4 kids and we share humorous stories about our children. Good night.

DAY 26: July 27
Oromocto to Point Wolfe Campground at Fundy National Park, N.B.

OMG! It feels wonderful to put on clean clothes! This little motel has a complimentary breakfast with – Yum! – Pancakes. I am a happy, clean, woman with a full tummy!

Last night I got on the Internet and booked a campsite at Bay of Fundy National Park. The only campground that had any sites left was Point Wolfe. It's at the far edge of the park on a dead-end road, paved, thank goodness. I think it will be perfect for me. Hooray for Camping!

Gorgeous day for riding. It's only a couple hundred km to the park so I take my time. Stop in Sussex to gas up and get groceries. It's always a bit of a movie to get groceries packed onto my already fully loaded bike. I have to spread out a tarp in my parking spot outside the store, untie my mini cooler, take the cardboard packaging off everything I've bought to conserve space, and try to fit as much as I can into the cooler. Of course it doesn't all fit – my cooler is the size of a six-pack! Then I start looking for little spots that I can cram things into inside my saddlebags – any crack or crevice will do. Whatever doesn't fit there gets tied on top with Teddy. It's a bit of a gong show!

And as usual I am a magnet for men over 75 years old. I talk with three of them; one at a time they amble over from different directions as I am packing. One of the gentleman is very sad and lonely. He got married, built a house, raised his kids and then his wife left him. "This is not how I planned my life," he said. "I have no-one to share it with." I feel sad for him.

Riding into Fundy Park, I can smell the ocean. It's been three and a half weeks since I left the west coast and I miss Mother Ocean. At the first viewpoint, I pull over and there she is! So so big and beautiful. I'm on a high cliff overlooking the Bay of Fundy and on the horizon I can just barely see the outline of Nova Scotia. Misty clouds float below me over the water. They call this area the "Land of Salt and Fir." That's what I can smell so strongly: the scent of the ocean and the trees mixed together.

I meet a lovely woman at the viewpoint. She has just immigrated to Canada from China. She's all bubbly and excited about life. I let her sit on my bike and take a picture of her with her camera; she wants a photo to send to her friends back home. She gives me a gorgeous silk scarf from China. Deep greens and blues; thank you.

I wind my way through Fundy Park and finally - Yes! This is Point Wolfe. The beach is only a short walk from my campsite. I set up my tent, decide dinner can wait, and stroll on down to the ocean. It feels good to just walk along the beach at sunset, looking for interesting rocks, smelling that wonderful salty smell and hearing the waves gently caress the shoreline. I think of a line from one of EE Cummings poems; "For whatever you lose, like a you or a me, it's always your Self you will find in the sea." I am home.

DAY 27: July 28
Bay of Fundy National Park, N.B.

Party animals camped in the site next to me last night; loud music, huge fire, talking and laughing. Just four people but it sounded like forty. I tried to be patient with them because I did the same thing in my late teens. But they are in their mid-twenties; they should know better. They are not mean or rude, just incredibly disrespectful of others.

But I had to draw the line when they started carving the bark off a birch tree between our sites to get their smoldering fire going.

"Hey," I yelled. "Don't do that! It's a living tree!"

"Oh," they replied, "Is it?"

"Yes," I screamed angrily, "and besides that, it's a birch. Birch trees are sacred to Shamans!"

They backed away from the birch tree. I'm sure they thought I was a crazy woman but I don't care. It's interesting that I won't speak up for myself, as in, "Could you be a little quieter please?" but I will instantly jump to the defense of a tree – "Don't mess with Mother Nature!"

It's a wonderful sunny day for a ride and I can just explore the area knowing that I am camping here again tonight. The ranger kicked the party animals out this morning, thank goodness.

I ride through the village of Alma and head down a secondary road along Cape Enrage. It meanders along the salt marshes next to the Bay of Fundy. The tide is going out and the sun causes a mist to rise from the wet marsh grass.

I find another secondary road called Point Mary. How can I not go down it with a name like that! There's an art gallery a little way along the road; they have amazing raku pottery inlaid with shells and stones. My favourite is a piece about two foot by one and a half feet ... it's a wall hanging with a mirror in it ... gorgeous swirls of blue and brown. As if it would fit on my bike – Ha!

I ride to Hopewell Rocks; this is what I came to see! They are incredible sculptures carved by the huge tides in the Bay of Fundy. At low tide they look like giant monolithic sculptures. At high tide the water goes up their narrow stalks to just below the bulbous heads. It's super busy at Hopewell Rocks with hundreds of tourists, but I walk down the beach a way and it's quieter with far less people. Seems like these magnificent sentinels have guarded this coast forever.

On the way back to my campsite, Ruby and I dance. It's been a while since we had the opportunity to do that. It's hard to dance on a road you've never been on before: you don't know the curves or the cant, where the bad pot holes are or which curves have gravel in them. But this is the same road I came out on; I'm just riding it from the other direction so I have a good idea of how it flows. I put pressure on the foot pegs, lower my center of gravity, and lightly counter steer with the handlebars. Awesome! Ruby and I weave around the potholes, lean into the curves and fly! So so so so so much fun!

Like last night, I decide dinner can wait and go for a walk down to the beach. It's very peaceful here. I sit on a log, listening to the waves lap against the shore. I notice what looks like a face in the cliff across the narrow tidal inlet. Is it a raven or a man? Or a man with a raven mask? Or a raven-man? I'm not sure . . . A raven flies low over the beach . . . I can hear the sound of his wings . . . Whoosh, whoosh, whoosh . . .

DAY 28: July 29
Fundy National Park to
Victoria Vale, Nova Scotia

Packed up my camping gear this morning and headed out. It's a bit of a long run today - over 400 km.

I stopped at the park info center to use their Wi-Fi. I was in there yesterday to write up a complaint about the party animals. And also, to get water: there's a plumbing malfunction at Point Wolfe and you have to go eight km to the info center to get water. Having to go so far for water is the pits, but it is what it is. It's the party animal situation that really bugs me.

I'm not trying to be a thorn in the park service's side; my whole point is to get them to be more proactive – they should patrol/supervise the campground at night so shit like this doesn't happen.

One of the guys I spoke to yesterday recognized me and asked, "Did my supervisor phone you?" When I replied "No," he got on the phone right away, called her and handed me the phone. Her name was Monica and she was awesome. She said that Fundy National Park is a family campground, incidents like this shouldn't happen, someone is assigned to patrol Point Wolfe and she would look into why no one was on duty that night. And she gave me a full refund! It felt good to finally be heard. Hooray for me for speaking up – I don't usually do that – except in defense of sacred

Birch trees!

Originally this weekend I was going to hang out with Kat in Halifax. At the last minute she got a music gig in New Brunswick. She phoned me and said, "But hey Mom, I was invited to a weekend BE-IN at a farm outside of Kentville. A lot of the people you met at Future Forest Festival will be there. I phoned Michel and Claudia and they said you are more than welcome to come. You'll like them, Mom. They're your age."

So here I am – at Michel and Claudia's picturesque little farm in the Annapolis Valley camped under an old apple tree in the orchard. I think I'll go jump in the hot tub now – Good Night!

DAY 29-30: July 30 - 31
VictoriaVale, N.S. – Michel
and Claudia's Farm

What an incredible place Michel has created! He has been here 35 years and his vision is to have a space where people can come to not only explore and discover themselves, but where people can come together and create "community."

This is not a commune – Michel and Claudia value their personal space. They are the only ones who live here permanently. They host events where large numbers of people come to attend workshops, learn from each other and create synergy.

What is the event this weekend? It's Michel's 63rd birthday! And he has asked Luc and Che to come and give a workshop on Human Design. Human Design is based on astrology and chakras; it's a way of understanding ourselves and others better so that we can support each other and work together more efficiently and creatively to accomplish our goals. Wow, that was a mouthful, but it's the best I can do to try to explain the Human Design concept.

As the day goes on more and more people arrive. Some are younger people who I met at the Future Forest – Greg and Riley and Gavin and Brad and John. Some are people my age from Halifax, Wolfville, and small towns in the Annapolis Valley. They are teachers, computer techies, musicians, small business owners, artists, physiotherapists, farmers; all walks of life are here; the commonality is a desire to have fun together and learn from each other.

Michel is very much a Leo – the lion king of the jungle. He is short, and like Shawn, Kat's boyfriend, reminds me of a Hobbit. He has an energetic and powerful personality, greeting everyone, hugging, laughing, teasing, subtly orchestrating the events of the weekend and making sure every individual feels warmly welcomed and has whatever they need.

He has invented a game called Folleyball. It's a combination of volleyball, ping-pong, and badminton. There's a net set up in a large grassy area outside his house. We use a rubber ball the size of a volleyball, but it's nice and light, almost like a beach ball. We keep score, but the game is fluid – teams can consist of one person or up to five or six people and sometimes the number changes during a match.

Like volleyball, you serve and then try to volley the ball back and forth over the net, scoring a point if the other team fails to return the volley. But there the similarity to volleyball ends and the "dance" begins. You can let the ball bounce once before you volley it back, like in ping-pong. You can hit the ball up to three times yourself or hit it to a teammate before you volley it over. You can hit the ball with your foot or head or hands or any body part. You can bounce it off the net or a tree. It's so much fun! There is a lot of laughter.

The fascinating part for me is watching Michel, his brother Mark, and some of the other guys who know the game well, as they play. They "dance" through the game; it's almost in slow motion; there is no rushing. They wait for the ball to come, let it bounce in front of them, hit it once, hit it again and then hit it over the net. It's their patience that fascinates me; the way they wait for it, then almost juggle the ball, then when it's perfectly aligned, send it flying back over the net. My tendency is to rush in and just volley it back. The thought occurs to me "What does this say about how we each approach life?" I prefer their fluid patient dance to my quick and not always effective response.

The "Oasis," Michel's farm, is a large property. A short walk from his house is a community area. There's a uniquely shaped building where workshops are held, and an open-air kitchen with a stove, fridge, sinks, counters and everything you need to cook for large gatherings. There's a stage and a dance area in the meadow and a huge fire pit surrounded by long wooden benches. There are numerous spots for tenting in amongst the trees.

As the sun sets, the music begins. Its electronic music like at Future Forest but more low key, danceable but softer. There are at least a hundred people here now, moving to the music, smoking pot, laughing, talking, and sharing. As the night goes on, the electronic music ceases and instruments come out: a guitar, bongos, a didgeridoo, a string bass, a trumpet, a mouth harp; the variety of instruments seems endless. Someone starts throat singing and others join in. It's an eclectic jam session that goes on well into the night.

It's hard for me to describe this experience. We are at our core social beings – we learn from each other. I find that for myself, I need time to commune with other people and then time to be by myself to process all the input. I need both in order to be in balance. Again, it's all about the "dance" and finding my own way of dancing through life.

DAY 31: August 1
VictoriaVale to Blomidon
Provincial Park, N.S.

Michel and Claudia and I sat for a long time on the grass under the apple tree this morning, talking about Human Design. In the Human Design system there are four types of Human Beings: Manifestors, Generators, Projectors and Reflectors.

Manifestors and Generators are energy beings. They have been on this planet for thousands of years. Think of the pharaohs as Manifestors and all their workers as Generators. Everything we have created in the world has been done by Generators, (art, music, literature, culture) but the direction of everything created has been controlled by Manifestors. Generators make up 70% of the population; Manifestors are 8%.

Most people you meet are Generators. They value home, family, and community. They love to give, to contribute, and to create and are happiest when they have work that is appreciated. They are grounded and centered.

Manifestors are the leaders. They can be good leaders like Teddy Roosevelt, concerned about others, or bad leaders like Hitler, into ego and power. Manifestors tell Generators what to do.

Just as human beings have evolved physically and mentally, we are also evolving spiritually/emotionally. Several hundred years ago, another type of human being appeared on this planet: Projectors. They are also leaders, like Manifestors. But, unlike Manifestors, they do not tell people what to do; instead they guide them. This is because Projectors are non-energy beings and in order for them to lead Manifestors and energetic Generators they must have their cooperation. They lead through consensus, community cooperation and role modeling. Other people give power to them. Projectors make up 21% of the population; Kat is a Projector.

And who are the last 1% of human beings? They are Reflectors. Reflectors have just appeared on Earth recently. Some people think they are not from this planet; that they came from somewhere else in the universe. They are non-energy beings like Projectors. Their chakras are all open; there is nothing solid about them; they are fluid.

Reflectors role is twofold: to absorb and understand and to mirror this back. A good example is at a community meeting when a heated issue is being discussed. The Reflector will calmly and succinctly reiterate the important points in order to provide clarity to the group. They are like a mirror.

Reflectors need to be aware that they are also like sponges – they absorb the energy of those around them. They can get lost and lose their own Self in other people's energy. They need to pull back and re-center themselves in the universe sometimes. Because their chakras are so open, they are curious about everything and are experiential learners. But they have to withdraw from society to process the multitude of input they receive in order to mirror it back.

I am a Reflector. None of us get to choose the role we play; it's given to us. It all seems very complicated to me and a very weighty responsibility. In order to accept my role and not feel overwhelmed, I have to simplify it.

How do I take all this information in and act on it? What is my purpose? How do I make the world a better place?

In simple language, I think my job is to see the "goodness" in other people and reflect that "goodness" back at them so that they can see their own wonderful beautiful Selves. Like a mirror, I'm not projecting anything, I'm only reflecting. But the reflection is powerful and awareness raising. Think of a candle reflected in a mirror and how much that increases the light.

In my simple mind, if I can just focus on the things I like about the other person, the rest will happen automatically. Most of the time that's easy. My challenge will be to take this philosophy of seeing goodness in others back into the real world of work and bills and schedules and sometimes negativity. All I can do is try ...

After this thoughtful, weighty, intense, but also enjoyable, conversation with Michel and Claudia, we hugged goodbye several times. It felt good to be back on the road with Ruby. Riding is so much easier than life – you just try to weave around the potholes!

I got lost several times even though I'm not going far. That's OK. The Annapolis Valley is a gorgeous place to get lost in. It has both of what I crave – mountains and ocean. I'm on the Bay of Fundy, on the Nova Scotia side this time, watching the tides roll in and out. Just my little tent and me camped on a hillside in Blomidon Provincial Park with a 180-degree view of the Bay. Life is good!

Maybe the journey isn't so much about becoming anything. Maybe it's about unbecoming everything that isn't you, so you can be who you were meant to be in the first place.

DAY 32: August 2
Blomidon Provincial Park
to Halifax, N.S.

No rush to get to Halifax until this evening; good, I can go exploring.

Blomidon Provincial Park is on the east side of Cape Split. When the tide goes out in the Bay of Fundy, the beach is miles of red sand. But the other side of Cape Split is a rocky boulder beach. Geological dichotomy. Cape Split is the home of Glooscap, a native spirit. He rattled my tent last night with the wind.

The west side of Cape Split is covered with those enormous black rocks that I love – they remind me of both Lake Superior and the west coast. Huge dark boulders imbedded in the shoreline, some rough and jagged, some smoothed by wind and waves.

I find a pirate haven; a structure built of driftwood and rope just above the high tide line. Driftwood benches and a table made of an old wooden spool equal a place to hang out and enjoy the view.

I so love the ocean and I so love the tides! And the tides in the Bay of Fundy are huge! I ride west down paved roads and gravel, finding small fishing villages, some touristy, some not. When the tide is out, there is no water at all in the harbours; the boats slowly nestle onto braces built into the harbour floor. Kind of like the cycle of life, rise and fall, up and down, in and out. We can either go with the flow or fight it . . . it's our choice.

DAY 33: August 3
Halifax, Nova Scotia

Hooray! I have finally arrived in Kat's stomping ground: Halifax.

I am staying at Coco (Mother Earth) and Nat's (mischievous

fairy) house. Coco is like the Mom here. The house is home to many people – James, Chelsea, Mariah, Phil, Kendra, Kat, and Shawn – some for a long time and some for a short time. I have my own little room with a big couch to sleep on. This is where Kat and Shawn stay when they are in town. They have kindly given me their space and they are staying at Blair's a few blocks away. They figure Blair's is too much of a party zone for me and, knowing Blair, I'm sure they are right.

Shawn has a plan for us today – we are going to the eastern shore to have lunch with his Mom so I can see where Shawn grew up. The eastern shore is about an hour east of Halifax and full of bays and inlets and tiny fishing villages.

Shawn's Mom, Marion, and her partner, Rusty, live in an adorable little house overlooking the bay. When I walk in, the smell of delicious food cooking makes me feel immediately welcomed. Marion gives me a big hug; she's all smiles and motherliness and just seems to emanate an aura of taking care of others. With her short blonde hair, gentle thoughtfulness and chatty conversation she makes me feel accepted and part of the family right away.

And, wow, her cooking is amazing! She works as a chef at a resort nearby and she loves to cook for people at home or at work. She enjoys playing with recipes and experimenting with new ideas and combinations. She serves us stir-fried vegies from her garden with rice and curry and little mushroom caps filled with sweet potato. Delicious!

Shawn's Mom has an idea for the afternoon – we're going to a beach to swim in the ocean. Sounds great to me; I haven't had a chance to swim in the Atlantic yet. The beach is incredible; hardly any people, white sand stretching indefinitely in both directions, waves gently lapping the shore. I am in my happy place.

Marion and I go for a long walk down the beach. The sand feels good between my toes. It's obvious that this is one of Marion's favourite places. We walk, we talk, we swim – the water is cold and refreshing and the sun is warm. She tells me about her life and Rusty and her two boys and how happy she is that Kat and Shawn are together. She is such a caring mom.

With lots of hugs, Marion heads home and Shawn becomes tour guide again. He wants to show me the cottage his great grandfather built where Kat and he stayed last winter. It's a short drive from the sandy beach. We come down a steep hill into a rocky bay dotted with islands and several fishing boats at the dock. Lobster and crab traps are stacked everywhere – hundreds and hundreds of them.

I can tell this is a special place for Shawn. It's where his roots are – as a kid he spent summers here, exploring amidst the rocks and the tide. He has kayaked in this bay scores of times and knows each of the islands intimately. He got his first job here working on a fishing boat, living for weeks out on the ocean. Shawn is part of this little harbor and it is part of him. I'm so glad he wanted to show this place to me.

And his great grandfather's cottage is full of memories. Its rundown and falling apart but you can feel the generations who lived here. Knickknacks from another era fill the walls and shelves, mixed in with found objects from the sea that someone carried home to excitedly share. It's a cozy place to just Be.

And then we head back to the city. It's almost like the car is a time machine linking the past and the present or a rocket ship which has taken us to another planet. I'm so happy that Kat and Shawn have shared this slice of their life with me!

DAY 34: August 4
Halifax to Battery Provincial Park, St. Peters, Cape Breton, N.S.

Another slow-motion morning – Do I know how to do it any other way anymore? I have a shower, do my laundry, load my bike, say goodbye to Coco and Nat and head over to Blair's to have brunch with Shawn and Kat. We go to a funky little café with excellent ham and eggs, smoothies and coffee.

Kat and Shawn are so cute together – they are both strong and independent, lovingly giving each other space to do their own things but also coming together in a powerful synergy. It's awesome to watch.

They are performing at a festival this weekend and won't be back into Halifax until next Monday evening. I decide its perfect timing for me to go spend a few days camping in Cape Breton and riding the Cabot Trail.

The 400km to Cape Breton goes fine until about half way. I come to a spot where the highway is closed because of a bad accident. The RCMP detours all the highway traffic, including me, down a secondary road for almost 100 km. Its three hours of stop and go ... stop ... go ... stop ... I've never been in a traffic jam this big for this long. It's a motorcyclist's worst nightmare. My clutch hand is killing me! There's no way out and nowhere to go. We are all stuck in this slow-moving parade.

Finally the detour ends and I'm back on the highway. I'm battling the setting sun now and I really want to find the campground I booked before darkness comes. I hate gravel roads in the dark and all campgrounds are gravel. I pull in an hour after sunset but there's still a wee bit of light. My campsite is on a high cliff overlooking the ocean. Amazing view! I have survived and arrived at my temporary Home Sweet Home.

DAY 35: August 5
Battery Provincial Park to
Highlands National Park,
Ingonish, Cape Breton, N.S.

Battery Provincial Park is such a beautiful campground! I wake up to a gorgeous view of St. Peter's Bay. Last night I fell asleep to the sound of the ocean. I am in my happy place once again.

It rained last night so my camping gear is pretty wet – not on the inside, just on the outside. It gives me an excuse to not pack up right away: I need to lay things out in the sun to dry. Not that I need a reason to go slow – I think "turtle" is my new spirit guide.

I hang out at the Park office for a while to use their Wi-Fi. Surprise! My friend Fred from Haida Gwaii is also at Cape Breton. I had forgotten that he was born and raised in Glace Bay at the eastern tip. We make arrangements to meet up tomorrow at one of the villages along the Cabot Trail. I'm curious to meet his new wife from the Philippines, Gigi.

Head out on the highway back toward the causeway, which links Cape Breton to the mainland, but instead of crossing it, I head northeast into the heart of the island. I'm going toward the northern tip, which is Cape Breton Highlands National Park. I've booked three nights in the park at two different campsites. On weekends, I always reserve campsites because they fill up, whereas on weekdays I just fly by the seat of my pants. I want to ride the Cabot Trail; it's famous for its scenic beauty.

And I am not disappointed. The Cabot Trail runs all along the coastline of the Cape Breton Highlands. I ride with the ocean on one side of me and steep mountains on the other. The road runs along deep fjords cut into the landscape with a tiny fishing village in the harbor at the head of every fjord. I cross translucent rivers with rounded red stones flowing to the sea. I love the curves in the road and so does Ruby. Where the land is too steep to make a road next to the shoreline, we climb mountains and do switchback after switchback. Ruby wants to dance and we do a little bit but I'm very aware of the numerous potholes, road snakes and dippsy doodles in the pavement. I don't know this place well enough yet to fly.

I arrive at my campground at Broad Cove and go to my campsite. What! There's no view of the ocean! I've been so spoiled lately with gorgeous scenic campsites that I forgot – not all campsites are right next to the water. Oh well, there's trees and birds and little chipmunks. It's all good.

I'm tired; I make something to eat and get ready for bed. I'm excited for tomorrow; there will be more mountains to climb, more fjords to ride along, more up and down and glorious curves, more opportunities for Ruby and I to dance ...

DAY 36: August 6
Cape Breton Highlands
National Park, N.S.

It's a bright sunny morning! I eat breakfast and put everything inside my tent, except what I need for a day of riding. I'm going to be staying here again tonight so it's nice to not to have to pack up my tent, to just have a day with no specific destination, a day for just wandering and exploring.

At the last minute, I strap Ted on my bike. I had put him in the tent, but then I heard him yell, "What! I came all this way with you and now you're leaving me here while you go enjoy the scenery!" He's right – it's not fair – I bring him along.

I stop at a cute little gift shop to see what they have. I can tell I'm going to be awhile and I charge my phone while I'm shopping. Oh! Up pops a text from Fred and Gigi. "We're in Pleasant Bay. We'll wait for you here." The message is an hour old. Whoops! I better get going.

Head down the road toward Pleasant Bay and make a wrong turn. (So what's new?) Pull over to think about it because I'm sure I'm going in the opposite direction that I should be. A guy pulls up next to me on a bike – "You lost?" he asks. "What was your first clue?" I respond. He laughs and tells me that, yes, I missed the turn off for Pleasant Bay but if I keep going in the direction I am right now, there's a beach that "You have to go see."

It's the way he said it – *You have to* - that convinces me to keep going. He rides ahead of me, slowing his pace to match mine, and when we get to the beach entrance, he stops briefly to smile and say, "You'll like it!" And rides on.

I do like it very very much. The tide is out and there are hardly any people on miles of red sand beach. I hang out for a little while and then phone Fred. It turns out that they are about 5 km away from where I am. If I would have skipped the beach and rushed to Pleasant Bay, I would have missed them . . . It's funny how things work out sometimes!

I meet up with Fred and Gigi at the corner right where I made the wrong turn – or the right turn as it turns out – and surprise! – They are riding on his Valkyrie. I had thought they were in his jeep. Big hugs. I haven't seen him for three years: not since I met him in Haida Gwaii and we went to the 4,000-year-old village of Ninstints on a float plane together.

Fred, Gigi and I ride until we find a café to have lunch. So much news to catch up on! Fred lived in Edmonton when I met him and now he's moved with Gigi to Moncton. His elderly mom is happy that he is finally back in the Maritimes. His whole family has lived in Cape Breton forever and his mother has never understood how he could move so far away.

Gigi is quiet and soft spoken, a beautiful Pilipino woman. She and Fred have been married for a little over a year. He calls her "angel" and you can tell he's madly in love with her. I remember when he posted their wedding on Facebook –they had only met a few months before.

In some ways it's hard for me to see Fred again: We shared incredible life changing experiences on Haida Gwaii. He has amazing blue green eyes that look right into your soul and he's one of the kindest, most thoughtful men I've ever met. If I could clone him I would. I really hope that he and Gigi live happily ever after.

Big hugs goodbye and then we set off in opposite directions. I head for White Point which is a favourite beach for locals. Ah yes, it's relaxing time! White Point is a small fishing harbor with about six houses and as many boats tied to the dock. But it also has a beautiful white sandy beach and the water is surprisingly warm. I go for a soothing swim in the salty ocean and lay on a big flat boulder out in in the water with the waves gently lapping at my feet. I feel like I'm a mermaid sitting on my rock surrounded by the sea. Feels good to get my gills wet.

White Point is a great beach for finding interesting pieces of driftwood. It's just the way the tide flows; some beaches are better for finding sea glass or agates but this is a driftwood beach. I meet a woman, Sharon, from Georgia who is also carrying a few interesting pieces. We compare our finds and talk about the faces and animals we see in each piece of wood. She has one that I name "Emergence" – it looks like a butterfly coming out of a cocoon. So good to talk with a kindred spirit!

By now I've been riding on this section of the Cabot Trail long enough that I know it better; the ins and outs, the ups and downs. When I had mentioned to Fred the enormous number of potholes and road snakes around here in his home stomping grounds, he laughed and said, "That just keeps the ride interesting!" OK; I can go with that perspective.

So Ruby and I dance. She loves this road. If I keep my center of gravity low, she finds her own way around the potholes and through the curves. We're dancing and flying at the same time, totally in sync with each other and the road.

And we're traveling through some of the most magnificent scenery in the world. We cut low into the fishing villages, inlets and harbours. We climb high over passes and switchbacks with stunning views where you can see for miles in all directions.

And almost everything is pink. The stones in the rivers are pink, the cliff faces are pink rock, the road is pink asphalt, and some of the sandy beaches are pink. No, I'm not wearing rose coloured glasses! It's almost like Mother Earth has opened and I can see inside her. Not like blood and guts or a wound; more like the pink inside your mouth or the palms of your hands . . . soft and vulnerable and warm. It's a good day to be alive.

DAY 37: August 7
Ingonish to Cheticamp, N.S.,
Along the Cabot Trail

The whole of Cape Breton is beautiful, but the Cabot Trail is the part that is extra special. Its only about 120 km long and runs between Ingonish and Cheticamp. Until the government decided to improve the road as a make work project in the 1930's, this area was extremely isolated. The same independent self-reliant families have lived here for umpteen decades.

I'm in no hurry to get to my campsite in Cheticamp – I have all day to just slowly explore as I ride there. While I'm washing my breakfast dishes, another camper mentions that there's a great beach at Black River where all the locals go. Sounds good to me.

But when I get there, the parking lot is totally full and the beach is wall-to-wall people. Maybe this is where the locals used to go, but obviously the tourists have discovered it!

Instead I go to Cabot Landing beach – the one that I made the wrong turn to yesterday – the one the guy on the bike said *I had to* see. It's incredibly beautiful: red sand stretching for miles and hardly a soul in sight. As I park my bike, a guy walks over to me. "Hey, aren't you the girl that I gave directions to yesterday?" I laugh and say, "Yes, and it's so beautiful that I had to come back!" We chat for a bit and then he goes off with his wife and I walk way down the beach to find a perfect spot to lay my blanket in the sun. By the way, it's not hard to find a perfect spot - any spot on this beach is perfect!

I'm hungry after swimming in the ocean and lying on the beach. (Whew! So much work!) I go back to the same café where I ate with Fred and Gigi yesterday. It's such a laid-back place and the waitresses are super nice. The walls and shelves are filled with ancient antiques; it's fun to just hang out and let your eyes explore while you're waiting for your food.

The waitress tells me it's nice to have me back again. I say loud enough for the cook to hear, "It's because the food is good and I like John Prine." The cook laughs; she's in charge of the music and she only plays old cowboy songs; John Prine is her favourite musician. It's the same album that was playing yesterday. Hey, as long as the cook is happy, I'm happy! She gives me extra ham, so I am definitely extra happy!

I keep traveling towards Cheticamp. Not in a hurry – just exploring and enjoying the views. This part of the Cabot Trail goes up and over three mountains. I know these mountains are not as high or rugged as the Rockies or the mountains in B.C., but they are millions of years older. This whole area was never part of the North American plate; it was connected to Africa along with Newfoundland, and was part of Pangaea billions of years ago. When Pangaea broke apart, Newfoundland and Nova Scotia floated away and banged into North America. The rock here is some of the oldest exposed rock on the planet – definitely worthy of respect.

So I respectfully ride it. Its foggy and misty this high up and I put on my rain gear. It doesn't rain, but I'm riding through the clouds and I can see and feel the moisture in the air. As I come over the last pass, the view opens and I watch the sun as it slowly sets into the ocean. Once again, it's a good day to be alive . . .

DAY 38: August 8
Cheticamp back to Ingonish, N.S., Along the Cabot Trail

I know, I know . . . Yesterday I went from Ingonish to Cheticamp . . . so how come the title for today's entry says "Cheticamp back to Ingonish?"

Well, you see, it's just too magnificent to leave yet. Instead of heading for Halifax, which was what I had planned on doing today, I text Kat – "Do you mind sweetie if I'm a day late?" "Of course not, Mom," she replies. "Have Fun!"

I head back the way I came from because I want to see the Cabot Trail again from the other direction. I want to cross up over those mountains again and feel Ruby and I gliding around those curves.

OK, there's another reason – I haven't mentioned Eric yet. Part of me wants to run away from him and the other part wants to learn more about him.

He's a biker; we met when I was camping at Cape Split and we've stayed in touch by text. When I tell him I'm on the Cabot Trail, he says, "Hey, do you mind if I meet you in Cheticamp? I've always wanted to ride the Cabot." I say, "Yeah, fine," figuring he may or may not show up; he's 400 km away and it's raining between here and there. But last night when I pull into the only gas station in Cheticamp, there he is! We go to dinner and out to the campground.

Eric is funny, serious, and kind of crazy. (But aren't we all a little bit crazy?) He's short, sort of round, with hair that is determined to stick out in all directions and green blue eyes with flecks of brown. It's his eyes that get to me: they're 3D and iridescent like marbles. When you look in his eyes you can see how warm his heart is. I know this could go sideways really quick, so I'm adamant that we each set up our own tent and sleep by ourselves in it. He's respectful; he doesn't try to convince me otherwise.

That's part of why I want to do the Cabot Trail again – to share it with him. So far I've done this whole trip riding alone; it's fun to have somebody to ride with, someone to share the adventure.

We go up over the mountains and take a break at "my beach." It's the third time I'm been to Cabot Landing; I figure I can call it "my" beach now. It's just as timeless as it was yesterday and the day before . . . and will be forever I'm sure. Its windy and the waves are pounding. We just lay on the red sand, sheltered from the wind and listening to the ocean. Thank God, Eric's the kind of guy that doesn't have to talk all the time.

We hang out on the beach for a quite a while and when we finally leave it's getting to be late afternoon. I'm not sure where we're going to camp because I hadn't planned on being in Cape Breton an extra day. We stop at a gas station in Wreck Cove to ask about campgrounds in the area. When I say we stop at a gas station in Wreck Cove, I should mention that the gas station is the ONLY building in Wreck Cove. It's a combination gas station, general store and coffee shop. The owners, Brent and Hope, are super friendly. They tell us they're from Ontario and they've been here four years. They came out to Cape Breton on a holiday, fell in love with the area, went home, and two weeks later saw the store for sale online, bought it and immediately packed up everything and moved. They live above the store.

Anyway, when I ask Hope about campgrounds in the area, she says the closest one is 50 km away, but that she's not sure if it will have any available sites because the weather has been so sunny that tons of tourists have been passing through.

She looks me right in the eye and says; "You know, its dusk now and it gets dark quick around here when the sun drops behind the mountains. That's when the moose come out on the road." She pauses, "How about if you just set up your tent under a tree in our backyard. I'd feel better – you'd be safer. It worries me to think of you on the road with the moose."

Brent, her husband, agrees. What incredibly thoughtful people! They give us a jug of water, firewood, and move their truck so the headlights shine where we set up our tents. They won't let us pay for anything. "If you need something, just holler," says Brent. "We're right upstairs."

Such a cozy spot. We can't see the ocean but we can hear the waves pounding against the shoreline. Eric and I sit by the campfire for a long time, talking and looking up in the sky – there are soooo many stars! You can see the Milky Way and a zillion constellations. We watch a shooting star fall right into the big dipper – Amazing!

DAY 39: August 9
Wreck Cove to Halifax, N.S.

Beautiful morning! Good sleep and I wake up to sunshine. And I don't have to make coffee – its already brewing in the General Store. Eric and I pack up, give Hope and Brent big hugs, and offer to pay for our spot; but they won't take any money so Eric puts twenty dollars into the jar they have for donations to the local Volunteer Fire Department. We hit the road; it's going to be 400 km to Halifax.

We ride and stop, ride and stop enjoying the views of the ocean and the mountains. Eric's not a "gas and go" kind of guy, thank goodness. We have a great ride all day. Stop here, stop there, chat about all kinds of things – the universe, negative/positive energy, people, ghosts, paranormal activity, the way spiritual and physical realms come together, how this affects our emotions, how our emotions affect our lives . . . Really good conversation. Eric rides with me to Coco and Nat's, hugs me goodbye and heads north 100 km to his home.

DAY 40: August 10
Halifax, Nova Scotia

Kat has planned another wonderful day for me in Halifax. "Hey Momma," she texts me in the morning. "Come for brunch with us. We're meeting up with Marion and Rusty." I'm happy to see Marion again; she's just so bubbly and happy and full of joy for life. Rusty is her handsome gentle musician husband. The conversation flows with lots of laughter between the five of us. We talk about lots of Mother stuff; like how we wish we knew (back when Shawn and Kat were little) all the things we know now about raising children. Hindsight is always 20:20, isn't it?

Marion gives me a beautiful shell necklace that she's made for me. It's a white sand smoothed shell she found on the beach that she has intricately wrapped with copper wire. She is very creative! She said, "I figured that you are like Kat in that you find beauty in plain and simple things rather than ornate and complicated ones." She got that right on. Marion has her own small business making jewelry from shells and stones and sea glass that she finds at the beach. Some are elaborately wired with pearls and crystals and beads. Others, like the one she made for me, are created to focus more on natural elements.

After brunch, Marion and Rusty head back home to the Eastern Shore. Kat says, "Grab your bathing suit, Mom, we're going swimming!" Kat and Shawn take me out to a fresh water lake that's less than half an hour from town. Big smooth flat rocks are embedded in the shoreline and gently angle into the water. It's warm and sunny and the water is clear and refreshing. We swim and float and dive underwater like dolphins. I like to dive down deep where the water is colder, holding my breath as long as I can, then when

I have no air left, bursting towards the surface like a seal or an otter. Love that feeling . . . It's so quiet under water . . . I wish I could hold my breath forever.

Kat and Shawn practice their "hooping" on the rocks. It's a great flat stage to perform on. I enjoy watching them "dance" with the hoop – it's a whirling balance - their bodies move slowly and rhythmically, while the hoop moves so quickly it's a blur. They try to teach me a few moves; I feel discombobulated and hopelessly klutzy. Kat laughs and says, "Its OK, Mom. We all hit ourselves in the face when we're learning!"

On the way home, I get a tour of Halifax. We drive past the different places that Kat has lived, and she shows me various neighbourhoods. We check out her favourite store, "Plan B", which is chock full of weird and wonderful new and used homemade stuff. I find a little wooden box imbedded with stones and a carved round wooden sculpture of a man and a woman. Kat tries on clothes made by one of her favourite fabric artists and, as is common for all female shoppers, she can't decide between two things she likes. I tell her that my solution to that problem is always just to buy them both! "But Mom, I can't afford both!" "OK," I respond. "Consider it an early Christmas present from me!" "But its only July!!" she exclaims. She certainly can be difficult sometimes. I give her a hug – "Merry Christmas, I Love You!"

DAY 41: August 11
Halifax, N.S. Touristy Tour

Another fun day with Kat and as usual she has a plan: we're doing the tourist thing today!

We go for brunch at a different place than yesterday; it's right on the harbor downtown. It's touristy but it's all organic food. Kat and I order a yummy kale omelet, and while we're waiting for it to be ready, we buy a liter of blue berries and basically just hoover them back. It's an appetizer, LOL! Feels so good to just sit by the water, eating and talking and drinking coffee.

Kat is very mature for a young woman. She is idealistic but at the same time grounded in reality. She tells me that yes, she knows that she and her friends live in a microcosmic bubble of creating a Caring Community, and she also understands that the rest of the world has a different perspective with a more economy based way of thinking. She is good at balancing her life between the two – holding in her heart her ethics and ideals and at the same time navigating through the real day-to-day world.

We go into several touristy shops; but we don't buy anything, it's just neat to look at all the souvenirs of Halifax. One shop is a bakery that specializes in rum cakes – the smell is to die for! If I could carry one on my bike without it getting squished, I'd buy it. Instead, Kat and I check out the tasting area – six times!

And then there's the ice cream shop; can't bypass that one and besides we didn't have dessert after brunch; the rum cake tasting certainly doesn't count as dessert. Again, we sit by the harbor chatting, this time enjoying our delicious cones.

Kat wants to have babies, maybe sooner, maybe later, with Shawn. She talks about home schooling and small independent community schools and how it's a common thing in rural Nova Scotia. But she's also aware that when her kids get to school age, she may have a different perspective on parenting than she does now. That's what I mean when I say she's idealistic AND grounded.

Kat has to leave before dinnertime; she has a music festival this weekend in Quebec and she and the three other performer friends are going to drive through the night to get there by tomorrow morning. Big hugs goodbye; I know I won't see her for many months and I love her so much!

I take myself for a ride out to Peggy's Cove to have some supper. It's a lovely gently curving road all along the coast. By the time I head back to Halifax, the sun is setting and the angle of the light makes the landscape glow. Big boulders crop out of the ground everywhere casting long shadowy reflections; and as always, there's that wonderful salty smell of the sea.

DAY 42: August 12
Halifax to The Ovens, just
south of Lunenburg, N.S.

Had to say goodbye to Coco and Nat this morning – they're such sweethearts: "Mary Jane," they told me, "you are more than welcome to stay at our place anytime." Big hugs to both of them and Chelsea and Mariah and James. They all share a caring communal space and wrap their light around everyone who enters.

Made an appointment at Privateers Harley Davidson to get a new front tire. My friend Don had told me before I left Vancouver that my tire wouldn't make the trip across Canada and back and to keep an eye on it. I have been and it was doing fine – until the Cabot Trail literally ate the tread off. I mean literally: the gravel and potholes chewed it right up.

There I sit with a 1:00 appointment and at 3:30 they are finally starting on my bike. Shit! I was planning on putting some miles on today – I have a reservation tonight at a campground a couple hundred km away.

I finally get out of the shop at 6:00. It's going to be dark in two hours. Eric and I motor. (Yes, I invited him to come camping with me on the south shore for a few days.) He's a good rider, interesting company, and he doesn't seem to mind that I like to stop at every viewpoint and tiny little one-horse town to check it out.

I've got to be careful with the new tire; the guy in the shop reminded me that new tires are slippery for the first hundred km. Whoops! I'd forgotten that. No weaving around potholes or leaning hard into curves until tomorrow. But it's OK to go fast.

Eric and I go very fast on the Expressway and slow down on the secondary roads. We're heading for "The Ovens," a campground that was recommended to me by a woman that I met on the Cabot Trail. I have to tell you a little bit about my conversation with this woman: It was another one of those "You have to go there" conversations.

She was describing the caves at the Ovens and the cliffs over-looking the ocean and how the rocks are in sideways stratified sheets and then she says, "But wait . . . Listen to this . . ." and she pulls out her cell phone. I'm totally confused; what does she want me to listen to on her cell phone? She has a video – well sort of, the picture doesn't change – of the rocks on the beach at the Ovens. It's the sound of the waves washing in and out that's mesmerizing. When the waves crash in, it's a sound that you hear on every beach – but it's the sound when the water flows back out that's so unusual . . . it's like the music of a hundred tiny little bells as the water causes the pebbles to jiggle and jingle against each other. That's why I have come to the Ovens . . . to hear the ocean sing.

DAY 43: August 13
The Ovens and Lunenburg, N.S.

And I am not disappointed . . . at the Ovens, the ocean sings all day and all night.

Our campsite is high on a cliff with the waves sometimes pounding and sometimes gently caressing the shore. The tide flows in and out changing the shoreline . . . at low tide, there are islands and peninsulas emerging from the water . . . at high tide they sink below the surface, covered by the sea.

And yes, the rocks are lying sideways in stratified sheets; layers of different deposits that were originally horizontal and were heaved upwards and turned so that now they point vertically toward the sky; ribbons of red, yellow, orange, gray, and brown rock. To say, "Its amazing!" feels like such an understatement.

Eric and I walk the trail that winds along the cliffs, exploring the various caves or "ovens." Why they are called ovens, I really don't understand. They are incredible caves formed by the pounding force of the ocean over millenniums. Each cave is different: some have a tiny opening to the ocean, others a large one. Whatever size, the water continually flows in and out.

You walk down sets of stairs cut into the rock, descending deep inside the caves. Inside some, the cave is large and round and tall. In others, it's long and narrow. In each one, the ocean sings a different song; it varies from a heavy bass booming echo to a whispering soft lullaby. Over and over again . . . an alluring melody.

As we walk, we meet other campers. We chat with a couple from Montreal who are bicycling across Nova Scotia. I tell them how much I admire their determination, because, yes, I'm on two wheels too, but I have a motor. He laughs and slaps his thighs and says he has a motor too! Another couple is from Ontario and they come to Nova Scotia every summer just to "amble;" they never know from one day to the next where they are going or what they are going to do; they just like to wander and explore in whatever direction the wind blows them. There almost seems to be a spiritual kind of bond between campers; we love to absorb the beauty and peacefulness of being outside surrounded by nature.

In the afternoon, Eric and I ride over to Lunenburg. I don't often enjoy cities, (too much traffic, tourists, hustle, and bustle) but Lunenburg is a special place full of history, colorful buildings, and funky shops. We park the bikes along the waterfront and walk up and down the hilly streets. There are tourists everywhere but it feels OK because I'm a tourist today too!

I love the colours of the buildings – fire engine red, fuchsia pink, lime green, neon orange, periwinkle blue, indigo purple and sunshine yellow. It's like a big box of Crayola crayons burst open and scattered everywhere. There are brightly coloured flowers in window boxes, gardens and hanging baskets that just seem to add to the sensory explosion.

One of the gift shops has a sign on the wall that says "The Rules." Eric and I laugh as we read them:

Rule #1: The Female always makes the rules.

Rule #2: The rules are subject to change at any time without prior notice.

Rule #3: No male can possibly know all the rules.

Rule #4: If the female suspects the male knows all the rules, she must immediately change some or all of the rules.

The list goes on in the same vein for a total of 15 rules. It's pretty humourous.

We're tired of gift shops and crowds so we find a little restaurant tucked off the main drag. A smiling Lebanese man who is obviously the owner greets us. "Hello Boss," he says to Eric. Having just read The Rules, I reply, "You must be talking to me!" "No," he says smiling with his eyes but not his mouth, "I'm talking to him – the man is the boss of the family!"

"Really!?!" I ask, "And what does your wife think of that?" "She knows," he says nodding his head sternly at me.

He takes us to a table out on the deck with a view of the Lunenburg waterfront. I ask him a few questions about different items on the menu. It's an eastern Mediterranean menu with various Greek and Lebanese dishes. He talks about where he gets his produce from (all local) and the different spices and herbs he uses. He's obviously very proud of his business and quality is important to him. When his son serves us, the food is arranged artistically on the plates. Quality and taste are always number one, but presentation can be equally as important. It's a family business: the owner is also the cook, his wife is the accountant, and his teenage children are the servers and dishwashers.

When we go to pay the bill, the owner's wife (of course) is running the cash register. I laughingly repeat to her our initial conversation with her husband. She raises her eyebrows, puts her hands on her hips and calls out to him through the door into the kitchen: "The man may be the head of the family but the woman is the neck – she tells the head which way to turn!" She speaks quite loudly but not angrily; and I see him nod, give her a half smile, and continue cooking. They may disagree sometimes about who is in charge, yet they obviously work together well as a family.

We take the scenic route back to our campsite at The Ovens. We curve around little towns and harbours, each one picturesque in its own quaint way. It's been a wonderful day; a nice combination of raw nature and manmade artistry.

DAY 44: August 14
The Ovens and LaHave, N.S.

Shit! I am a good camper but I totally blew it last night.

It's raining when I wake up. I don't even want to get out of my tent. It rained hard all night; as a matter of fact, it rained real hard. I'm dry in my sleeping bag but when I peek out of my tent flap what I see is a disaster.

I had piled all our extra gear, including my biking boots, under the picnic table and put a tarp over the top of the table to protect everything from the morning dew. But I made two mistakes: 1. I didn't put rocks on the tarp to hold it in place; it's blown off and is lying in the grass in a wet heap. 2. I didn't notice that the picnic table is sitting on a low spot. There is a large puddle under the table now – with all our gear half submerged in it!

Thankfully the sun comes out and we spend a couple hours unpacking wet bags full of sopping wet gear and hanging it out to dry. I pour the water out of my leather boots and attempt to dry them in the sun. Oh well, it is what it is.

Yesterday we explored the area east of The Ovens, including Lunenburg. Kat and her friends had told me about some places west of The Ovens, including LaHave, which I want to check out today.

I put on my still wet boots (squish, squish, squish) and Eric and I head out on the bikes. LaHave is across the inlet from us – a ten-minute ferry ride – but instead we decide to go all the way up the inlet and down the other side. Definitely the long way around but the sun is shining and I just feel like riding. It's a gorgeous road along the inlet; curvy, well paved, little villages and harbours, fishing boats moored at the docks and "painted ladies" looking out onto the water. Scenic, relaxing, pretty and the perfect place for Ruby and I to dance.

We pull into LaHave, which is only three or four buildings, and go into the bakery/craft shop/library. It's the bakery that Kat and her friends rave about. The building is over a hundred years old and was originally a mercantile store selling supplies to fishermen and homesteaders. The smell of homemade bread nearly knocks you off your feet when you walk in the door. Even if you weren't hungry when you got there, your taste buds are salivating as soon as you enter. We order sandwiches and coffee and take a look around while we wait for them to be made.

The bakery is kind of an eclectic mix of the past and the present. There are homemade jams and pickles and all kinds of pastries for sale, and of course bread. The walls are full of pictures of the building when it was a mercantile business and there's shelves of old tools of the trade; a typewriter, a scale, a huge iron safe and other interesting stuff.

There's a local craft store under the bakery. I try the door, but darn, it's locked, they're closed. I peer through the windows at all the beautiful items. I see a woman sitting at the cash register and when she looks up, I gesture, "Are you Open?" She shakes her head "No" but comes to the door and unlocks it. "We're closed" she says, "but I've got about fifteen minutes of bookwork to do, if you want to come in and look around." YES! I pick out a few things I like, pay her cash, and comment on what a beautiful artists co-op this is. She smiles – she's one of the artists.

Eric and I ride over to the ferry to go across the inlet back to The Ovens. It's a little twelve car ferry that runs every half hour. Back and forth, back and forth all day, it lets tourists and locals shave hours off their driving time. It reminds me of the little ferries we have in B.C.

We arrive back at The Ovens just in time for a concert in the tiny canteen there. I had reserved a table for us yesterday because I knew the concert would sell out. Harry Chapin was a famous musician in the 70's; "Cats in the Cradle" was a hit then. He has passed away but his family owns The Ovens campground and they are all musicians. One of his brothers is playing the piano, another on guitar, and two nieces are the vocalists. Harry's Mom is holding a great grandbaby on her knee bouncing her in time to the music.

777

The music is exceptional; they play some of Harry's songs and some of their own. The young women's voices blend in a sweet harmony that when you close your eyes makes you think of angels.

DAY 45: August 15
The Ovens to Yarmouth, N.S.

It's a happy day but a sad day too. You know that bittersweet feeling? That's what it's like. I'm happy because I've had such an amazing time getting to know and explore Nova Scotia but I'm sad because this is my last day in this incredible province. Well, I'll just have to make the most of it.

Last night after the concert, Eric and I went for a long walk out on the rocks in front of our campsite. The tide was low and we walked way out on a peninsula that only appears when the water recedes. It was wonderful to listen to the ocean sing its own lullaby with the water lapping against the rocks. The pebbles tinkled like bells as the waves moved them in and out of the crevices in the boulders. Got my boots wet again in a couple of tide pools that I didn't see in the dark. Oh well, I'd do it all over again just to hear the ocean sing.

Packed up the bikes and rode out heading west. I reserved a hotel in Yarmouth for tonight because I need to be on the six-hour ferry to Portland, Maine at 7:00 am tomorrow morning.

Stopped at the LaHave bakery again for breakfast. It's impossible to drive past that place without stopping – the smell draws you right in. Sat on the front porch devouring delicious sandwiches and chatted with a local couple. They had just spent the past three years in Dubai. He works in the oil industry and she is a teacher. I really enjoyed talking with her about teaching overseas: how it's the same but different from teaching in Canada. She had fourteen different nationalities in a class of thirty students! She taught Grade 1 (all in English) but the kids also had to take Arabic (another teacher came in to teach that). She said it was a great experience and she highly recommended it. Hmmm, food for thought . . .

The couple in LaHave told us about a beach a few miles down the road at Cherry Hill that only the locals go to. There's no signage saying, "Beach" so it's not a place that tourists ever find. "Just turn left on the gravel road next to the fire station and keep going until it dead ends," they said. Sounds good to me.

The gravel road is not bad and at the end of it we park in the little turn around with a few cars. We climb over a sand dune and an incredibly long sandy crescent shaped beach spreads out before us. Nirvana! We walk for a while and then sit in the sand watching the waves.

It's an amazing spot – we are sitting at the apex of the crescent shaped beach so the waves are breaking on both sides of us. As they break, the crests run towards each other and then they "POOF" up in the air when they hit. I don't know if I can describe it any better; I've never seen anything like this before. I watch it over and over again – wait for it, wait for it – then poof – the breaking waves from each side collide together in an upward spray of lacy foam. Incredible!

Of course I have to go for a swim in the ocean. The water is not too cold and the waves are big enough for body surfing. The sandy bottom feels soft as I wiggle my toes into it. I pretend I'm a little dolphin gliding through the waves, letting them push me towards the shore on their crests; then turning around, I dive under them to get deeper and then resurface to do it all over again. It's a good way to say goodbye to the Atlantic. I swim until my teeth are chattering and then lay on my towel in the sunshine on the warm sand.

And, yes, we spend too long at the beach and we need to really motor if we're going to get to Yarmouth before dark. We take the highway, which in this area is just a two lane well-paved road with a passing lane added now and then. It's all good, we can do 110 kmph most of the way.

Stop in Liverpool for a quick coffee at Tim Horton's and then keep going. It's dark, very dark, by the time we get to Yarmouth.

Stop for gas, so that I'll be all ready to ride to the ferry in the morning. Reach for my wallet – it's not in my pocket where I always put it. Check my other pockets – no wallet. Take off my coat, empty all my pockets – no wallet. Check my pant pockets, my purse, and my saddlebags – no wallet. Shit! My stuff is spread out on the pavement all around my bike at the gas station as I search through everything for my wallet. It looks like I'm having a yard sale.

The last place I used my wallet was in Liverpool at Tim Horton's so I phone them to see if someone found it and turned it in. No luck. I ask the young man I'm talking to if he would please go out and check where I parked my bike. Maybe it fell out of my pocket there. He puts me on hold and goes out to look – no wallet. I give him my phone number just in case someone finds it and turns it in.

What am I going to do now? I have my passport so I can get across the border on the ferry which is already paid for, I have a place to sleep tonight since the motel is already paid for too, but I have no drivers license, credit card or debit card, and only about $60 in cash. That is not enough to get me to Michigan where I know my Mom will loan me some money. Eric offers to go to a bank machine and take out several hundred dollars. I don't want to borrow money from him, but it's the only solution I can think of.

It's late and I'm tired and upset. I pick all my stuff off the pavement and pack it back on my bike. I decide to go to the motel, check in, and then start making phone calls to cancel my credit/ debit cards. I don't want to sit at this gas station any longer and I know I'll be on the phone for a while canceling cards. I'd rather do that in the comfort of my motel room instead of sitting on a curb at a gas station.

When I get to the motel, I notice there are a couple messages on my phone. Maybe they're from Tim Horton's – hope, hope, hope - but they're not. They're from a police officer in Liverpool. He tells me that a young woman found my wallet at Tim Horton's and brought it to the police station. He says, "It's obvious that

you're a traveler from BC by your drivers license and you definitely need your wallet. I went to Tim Horton's and they gave me
your phone number. Phone me, I'd like to get your wallet back to
you."

Oh good! Oh good! Oh good! I phone Officer James back and
thank him. He asks if I'm still in the area and I reply, "Unfortunately no. I'm in Yarmouth because I have a ferry reservation
early tomorrow morning." In my head, I'm thinking that I'll have
to cancel my $200 nonrefundable ferry reservation, drive several
hundred km back to Liverpool tomorrow, get my wallet, and then
drive back to Yarmouth, and take the ferry the next day. Officer
James says, "Let me see what I can do; I'll phone you back." I have
no idea what he has in mind.

Officer James phones me back. By now it's after midnight. He
says he's driving my wallet to the county line where he will pass
it on to another police officer in that county, who will drive it to
the next county line and pass it on to the Yarmouth police. He
asks me what motel I'm staying at; the Yarmouth police will deliver my wallet to me there.

I'm so grateful that I'm almost crying. I mean he could have just
said, "We'll hold your wallet in Liverpool until you get here tomorrow." But he didn't – he bent over backwards to help me catch
my ferry and get on my way. I thank him profusely and he modestly replies, "It's just part of my job."

At almost 2:00am the police officer in the second county
phones me. He explains that the Yarmouth police are busy with
a traffic accident and could I meet him at the county line? I hesitate, "I'm on a motorcycle," I say "and . . ." He interrupts me immediately. "Oh, you can't be riding on the highway at this time of
night," he says. "There's too many deer. I'll deliver your wallet to
your motel. I'll be there in about half an hour." I thank him several
times.

Officer Smith arrives at my motel and phones me to let me
know he's outside. I can't stop thanking him when he hands me
my wallet. I'm so grateful, I want to hug him but I figure that
would not be appropriate. I can imagine the headlines in the local

paper, "Woman dressed in pajamas hugging police officer outside motel room at 3:00am." Instead I tell him how much I appreciate Officer James and himself and how grateful I am that they went so far out of their way to help me. He smiles and says, "It's our job to help people."

I'm tired but happy. Things could have gone sideways at any point in this sequence of events. But instead, I have my wallet and I'm still going to make the ferry in a few hours. Thank you God, thank you Universe, thank you Officers James and Smith!

PART III: YARMOUTH, N.S. TO VANCOUVER, B.C.

Map 3: Yarmouth NS
to Vancouver BC

#32. Yarmouth NS: Day 45
#33. North Conway NH: Day 46
#34. Johnstown ONT: Day 47
#35. Milton ONT: Day 48
#36. Brighton MI: Day 49-52
#37. Mackinaw MI: Day 53
#38. Marquette MI: Day 54-55
#39. Grand Rapids MN: Day 56
#40. Devils Lake ND: Day 57
#41. Williston ND: Day 58
#42. Glasgow MT: Day 59
#43. Shelby MT: Day 60
#44. Kalispell MT: Day 61
#45. Creston BC: Day 62
#46. Balfour BC: Day 63-64
#47. Greenwood BC: Day 65
#48. North Vancouver BC: Day 66

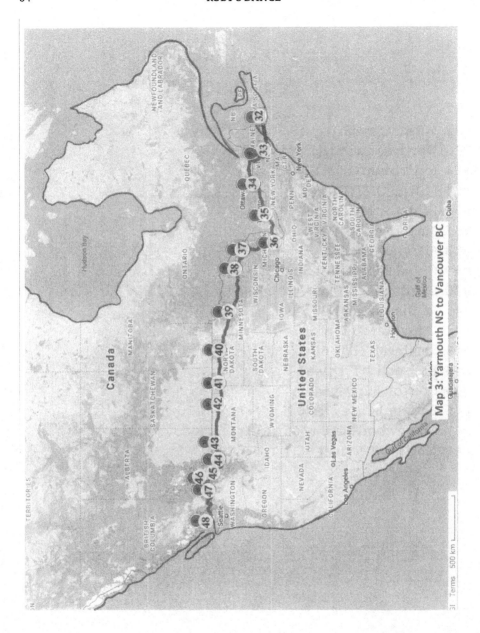

Map 3: Yarmouth NS to Vancouver BC

DAY 46: August 16
Yarmouth, Nova Scotia
to Portland, Maine
to North Conway, New Hampshire

I don't do well on 3 hours sleep. My eyes are open but my brain is not functioning. I say goodbye to Eric, get Ruby and myself on the ferry, find a couch and curl up and go to sleep.

It's an open water crossing and there's not much to see when I wake up. But all the little buoys in the water amaze me. I ask someone what they're for and they inform me, "Lobster Pots." But how do the fishermen find them? "By GPS," they reply, and add, "No idea how they found them in the olden days." Me neither. There's just water for 360 degrees around the horizon.

The boat docks in Portland, Maine and I have to go through immigration. I tell the officer that I'm a U.S. citizen and a Canadian landed immigrant. "So," he says abruptly, "Are you entering the U.S. as a U.S. citizen or Canadian?" Is he messing with my head? I've handed him my U.S. passport, I've told him I'm a Canadian landed immigrant and I know you can't enter another country using landed status, only by using citizenship status. "I'm entering the U.S. as a U.S. citizen." I reply. "Tell me," he demands, "What is a U.S. citizen doing with a Canadian registered motorcycle?" Now I'm getting really confused. I explain for what feels like the third time that I'm a U.S. citizen, a Canadian landed immigrant and I live in North Vancouver, B.C. It says all that on my passport and he's looking right at it. He reluctantly lets me go. Gee whiz – he sure got up on the wrong side of the bed! Or maybe I'm just overly sensitive and grouchy from lack of sleep.

The ferry has docked right in downtown Portland. I manage to find my way out of town and onto the highway without getting lost. I consider this an outstanding accomplishment since on a lot of days I feel that I couldn't navigate my way out of a wet paper bag.

It's not really a highway that I'm on, more like a two-lane road with lots of traffic lights. In this part of Maine, the mountains run north/south and so do the roads unless you go south to Boston where you can pick up the westbound interstate. I am not going south – I'm heading north and hoping to jog west and then north again. (Nancy, if you're reading this I know you are shaking your head – you are far better at planning ahead than I am!)

There is construction and detours and traffic and then it starts to rain. I persevere for a couple hours. Finally I come to a major tourist town where traffic is at a total stand still because of an accident. I'm wet, cold and tired from lack of sleep. My clutch hand is aching from all the slow speed stop and go. As much as I want to get into White Mountain National Park just on the other side of North Conway, I realize that I'm done.

I see an Info Center a block ahead and I park and go in. I apologize to the woman behind the counter for dripping all over her floor and ask if there are any inexpensive motels close by. This is a tourist town and I imagine accommodation will be expensive. She's very kind, recommends one a couple blocks away that's $100 U.S. a night. I know I have to take it – I really am in no shape to go any farther.

The motel is fine: not fancy, but it has a hot tub and a pool and a little restaurant next door. The restaurant is closed for the night already but I go to McDonalds across the street and get a McLobster burger. Who knew McDonald's made lobster burgers? I soak my weary bones in the hot tub, float in the pool, crank the heat up in my room and lay out all my wet gear to dry. Tomorrow will be a better day.

Just a note about Eric: It was fun and now it's done. Hey, I'm a poet and don't know it! I think he was hoping for something more between us but that didn't happen and it's not going to. He's got his life and I've got mine at opposite ends of the country. We had the opportunity to share some really great adventures together exploring the Cabot Trail and the South Shore.

If I believe that everyone we encounter in our lifetime has

something to teach us, what did I learn from Eric? And how does this tie in to what I learned about Human Design from Michel and Claudia and being a Reflector? I'm not sure . . . I haven't put all of the pieces of the puzzle together yet.

I just know that people's lives are complicated and the more you get to know them, the more complicated they appear. Supposedly my purpose as a Reflector is to be a mirror for others to provide them with clarity about themselves. I don't know if I do my job very well. I just know that I have to be careful not to get so involved that I lose myself. The only Self I have is my own.

DAY 47: August 17
North Conway, New Hampshire to Johnstown, Ontario

I feel much better when I wake up. It's not raining anymore but the sky is leaden with low hanging clouds. I have a lovely breakfast at the little restaurant next door, (breakfast comes with the $100 room, thank goodness) and put on my rain gear and hit the road.

Lots of cute little shops in this town and, I realize as I drive through, North Conway is a ski town just like Whistler. No wonder accommodation is so expensive! I don't stop to check out the shops because I really want to try to make some mileage today to make up for yesterday.

The drive through White Mountain National Park is beautiful: curvy road, well paved, mountains going way up into the clouds, big cliffs, lots of rivers. Some sun would be nice but at least it's not raining.

Cross the border just southeast of Montreal. The Canadian border guy is super friendly. He has a motorcycle too and we chat for a few minutes about road trips and great places to ride. "Welcome back to Canada," he says, "Enjoy the rest of your trip." It's obvious that riding coast to coast is something he would also enjoy doing someday.

I hit the outskirts of Montreal just as afternoon rush hour is starting. Super bad timing. There's construction, signage is terrible, and where there is signage, it's all in French. I get lost twice and end up in downtown Montreal both times – in Rush Hour! I have to keep pulling over to use my cell phone for GPS.

I think about giving up and phoning my friend Luc. I know he's visiting his family in Montreal and he's already said I would be welcome to stay with them. But I don't want to stay in the city – I want to get to the nice campground in Johnstown Ontario that I stayed at a month ago on my way east.

So I keep going. Getting lost in Montreal has waylaid me by two hours and its getting dark, but as I finally get back on a westbound highway (I'm not fussy about which highway anymore, just one that goes west please), there's a full moon rising.

I make good time and I know that Greenwood Campground is just off the 401. I didn't realize that it was 600 km from North Conway. That's way more mileage than I usually do in a day. (Whoops, lack of planning again.)

But look – there's signage from the highway exit right to the campground – and it's in English! Hooray for Ontario! And I get the same campsite I had last time ... And the full moon is shining over the St. Lawrence Seaway ... And my neighbours Melissa and Ross invite me over for a beer ... Oh yeah ... Life is Good!

DAY 48: August 18
Johnstown to Milton, Ontario

What a gorgeous morning! Sunshine, the St. Lawrence Seaway right in front of my camping spot, ducks swimming in the water and seagulls flying overhead. I am really moving slow this morning. I woke up super early and watched the sunrise over the water. And then I went back to bed!

Stayed up late last night chatting with Melissa and Ross. They are a wonderful couple with four super nice kids. They live on an acreage outside of Ottawa and you can tell their kids are country kids; they're comfortable chatting with anyone of any age because that's what you do in the country – gatherings are always family oriented and include everyone from babies to grandmas.

Ross says they do a lot of camping. Melissa tells me that when they're home in the summer, they leave their tent trailer set up so their kids' friends can come for sleepovers and hot dog roasts and, of course, some-mores! Fun times!

I debate with myself whether I want to have a morning swim or take a shower. Hmmm, if I have shower I can wash my hair, which badly needs it, but the seaway looks inviting . . . I can't resist . . . I go swimming with the ducks.

It's really hot and I leave my bathing suit on while I pack all my gear on Ruby. My wet bathing suit keeps me cool. I change into riding gear and within three minutes I'm covered in sweat. Oh well, the wind on the road will cool me off again.

I head to Gananoque. I had to rush through this area on my way east but now I have time to enjoy exploring it. The Thousand Island Parkway is a beautiful road that hugs the shoreline of the St. Lawrence and passes through several small towns with the most charming old houses I've ever seen. They're incredibly quaint and wonderfully kept up. There are little shops full of weird and wonderful antiques and things. Only the fact that I can't possibly fit any more stuff on my bike keeps me from going on a shopping spree.

I notice a Craft Market happening on the lawn of the county building in Gananoque. More weird and wonderful things to see and to eat! I devour an entire liter of fresh raspberries while I'm waiting in a line up to buy a homemade Brie and walnut loaf of bread. Yum to both!

By now its 4:00 and I've only gone 70 km. Well at least it will be after rush hour when I hit Toronto. I plan on camping at Milton campground which is west of T.O. I'm looking forward to having a glass of homemade Portuguese wine with Fernando and Anne who I met there a month ago.

Traffic is OK even around Toronto. Its heavy, like it is around any city, but people are at least driving sanely – unlike Montreal where I swear they are all crazy!

And then it gets dark ... and then it starts to rain ... and then it rains harder. I can't pull over, the shoulder is not wide enough, it just wouldn't be safe. So no, I can't stop to put on rain gear. I know I'm getting close to Milton and I don't want to accidently take an exit that doesn't have an entrance back onto the freeway just to rain suit up. As the rain drips down the front of my leather jacket and pools on the seat, I can feel it coldly soak into the crotch of my jeans. I hate that feeling.

I take the Milton exit and stop at the first gas station I see. I can't remember exactly where the campground is and I really don't want to be driving in circles in the rain. There's a customer and his son talking to the owner. I ask the owner for directions to the Milton campground. The customer looks at me. "Where you from?" he asks. "B.C." I say. "You rode here from B.C.?" I nod. "By yourself?" I nod again. "And you're camping?" I nod again. He looks outside. "In the rain?" he asks incredulously. I reply with a smile, "You know what they say about Vancouverites? We all have webs between our toes." He laughs and shakes his head. It's OK if some people think I'm crazy - they seem to like me anyway. (I think they do anyhow).

Finally arrive at Milton Campground in total darkness. The night watchman is very accommodating. He gives me the same campsite I had before and guides me down the gravel road with his golf cart; I can see the dips and doodles with his headlights. He puts a piece of board under my kickstand so my bike won't sink into the rain soaked ground. He says, "Just register in the morning. Don't worry about it now." I set up my tent and crawl into my warm dry sleeping bag. Ahhh ... Good night!

DAY 49: August 19
Milton, Ontario to Brighton, Michigan

Yay! When I wake up the rain has stopped and the sun is shining. Thank you God! I lay out all my extremely wet gear on four unused picnic tables. There are no other tenters in the campground (Duh, I wonder why? . . . Maybe no one else has webs between their toes.)

Fernando and Anne wander over and give me big hugs. "We thought we heard a motorcycle pull in late last night," they say. "We had no idea it was you!" They invite me over to their camper for coffee and even though I want to pack up and make some miles today, I know I will really enjoy chatting with them again.

Anne is such a sweetheart. She makes me a coffee and asks me about my trip. I wax prolific about how much I love Nova Scotia. It brings back tons of memories for her; I had forgotten that she grew up just outside of Halifax. We talk about the Bay of Fundy and its enormous tides, the Cabot Trail and the pristine vistas from the tops of the mountains, the Southern Shore and its amazing sand beaches.

She gets really excited and puts the idea out to Fernando that maybe instead of spending their summers in Ontario they could spend them in Nova Scotia. I mention that I met several couples who, like them, go to the southern states in the winter but lease a seasonal spot for their campers in the summer on the South Shore in Nova Scotia.

Fernando is reluctant. Ontario is a known item to him; Nova Scotia is not. Anne and I start talking about the abundance of artists and musicians in Nova Scotia: the spur of the moment jam sessions that magically occur when musicians get together, the artists guilds and co-ops in almost every little harbor, the spirit of community and cooperation between creative people.

Fernando's eyes light up. He is both an artist and a musician and he is hungry for that kind of community. It's been lacking in his life the past few years and just talking about it makes him aware of how much he yearns for it. By the time I leave, he's on the same page as Anne. Next summer he wants to be by the ocean again surrounded by fellow artists and musicians. (Remember, he grew up in the Azores – he's got a saltwater soul!)

When we part, I feel like we are old friends. It's good to be with people who I've met and enjoyed chatting with before. It's nice to be with kindred spirits who love the ocean and music and art and who are old enough to remember being in our twenties and going to music festivals and sharing whatever we have with others.

In a lot of ways being retired is like being in your twenties. There's a sense of freedom, a minimum of responsibilities, you're not tied to a clock or a calendar. You live every moment to the fullest, partly because you just might die tomorrow. There's a song with a line in it: *Don't ask her why she needs to be so free . . . She'll tell you it's the only way to be.* That's how I feel right now.

It's such a beautiful day! I pack up, hop on my bike, big waves to Fernando and Anne and hit the highway. I feel like I'm homeward bound - heading west. I'm not sad anymore about leaving Nova Scotia. Life is just one big continual adventure.

I'm excited to see my Mom and brother and sister again. My Mom's house is home away from home for me. There are pictures of all of us growing up on the walls and pictures of the grand-kids and memories of all the fun, amazing, incredibly good times we've had together.

My sister Nancy is at Mom's house to greet me. We're having a sleepover again! It's like when we were little, sharing a bedroom with twin beds. It feels good to be home. I love you both.

DAY 50: August 20
Mom's House and
The Howell Melon Festival

Ahhh! It is awesome to sleep in a real bed again! So nice to be at my Mom's house with her and my sister. I feel like I'm in a warm cozy place surrounded by love.

My Mom is without a doubt the best Mom in the entire world. I know she worries about me and yet she's always supportive in all the slightly crazy things I decide to do. I don't know if she knows how brave and independent she is herself and that I am actually just taking after her. When I am my Mom's age, I hope that I am just as excited about life and wanting to try new things and explore new places as she is. I love and admire her so very much!

Today, my brother John, my sister Nancy and my Mom and I are going to the Howell Melon Festival. Brighton (where Mom lives), and Pinckney (where John lives), and Howell are all small little towns that are close together and surrounded by farmland. Howell is famous for the cantaloupes they grow, hence the melon festival this time of year when the melons are ripe.

It's just the right size of event for me, not too big and not too small. Howell is only a few blocks long and the main street is closed to traffic so that craft booths and food venders can set up all down the middle of the street.

We look at stone jewelry and glasswork and imports from Ecuador. The guy from Ecuador notices that my earrings are abo-riginal and asks where I got them. I tell him a Mi'kmaq artist in Nova Scotia made them and he nods. There's a bond between Indi-genous Peoples around the world that I as a white Caucasian will never fully understand. I can appreciate it, but never be part of it.

My brother and I watch the dog show for a while. My brother loves dogs and he really gets a kick out of watching them. There's a large swimming-pool-size tank of water with a long raised plat-form next to it. The owner holds the dog at one end of the plat-form; a trainer shows the dog a toy, then races to the other end of the platform and tosses the toy high into the air, just as the owner releases the dog. The dog leaps off the platform into the water to retrieve the toy. Then he climbs a ramp out of the water to enjoy a big wet hug with his owner.

It was fun to watch the dogs who had never done it before. My brother and I laughed and laughed. When their owners released them, they would race to the end of the platform and then come to a screeching halt just before the water. They'd run back and forth at the end of the platform like they were saying, "I want that toy, I really want that toy, but I don't want to go in the water!" Eventually they would reluctantly jump in to retrieve the toy. The dogs always caught on after the first attempt; then they would show their prowess and leap way way up trying to catch the toy in mid-air before it hit the water.

Since it was such a hot sunny day, I challenged my brother to a water balloon fight. He didn't want to at first, but when I teased him about thinking he was so sweet he would melt, he agreed. Big slingshots were set up and you could really fire the water balloons at each other. I got him sooo wet - he said I only won because I'm short - Yeah, right!

There were lots of restaurants on the main street but we decided it'd be more interesting to eat festival food. We got Italian sausages from one stand, lemonade from another, and kettle corn from another stand. Yum! Found an empty table to sit at to eat and watch the festivals goers pass by.

It was great to sit and talk with my Mom and brother and sister and enjoy the festival. It was the kind of thing we used to do when the three of us were kids with my Mom, a short 50 years ago. Blast from the past; good memories! We talked about the holidays we used to go on together (lots of camping trips), the places we went to, and the things we remembered from them. Each of us had different memories; lots of stuff my brother and sister remembered were things I had forgotten until they mentioned them. Interesting that what stood out for each of us was the same and yet from a slightly different perspective. All good, all tied to happiness and lots of laughter.

My sister Nancy had to work in the evening but John's wife Nancy (sometimes it's confusing to have two Nancys in the family) came with John, my Mom and I to a dinner theatre in Pinckney. I hadn't been to a dinner theatre in eons.

Dinner theatres are awesome. Our waiter was the director of the play and two other waiters were the actors. They were the only two actors in the play, but they played twenty different characters! Sometimes they were a man, sometimes a woman, sometimes young, sometimes old, but always hilarious! The play took place in the Texas town of Tuna and it was outrageously funny. I don't know how the actors managed to keep their characters straight; every character had a different voice, a different walk, a different personality, and of course a different costume. It was a very humorous portrayal of the lives of the residents of a

to do myself." Now he is buried here too and so is my Dad.

I'm sorry I missed my Dad's funeral. You never get advance notice that someone is going to die. I had work commitments that I felt I couldn't put aside. In retrospect, I should have gone and let the chips fall where they may at work. At the time I thought, "It doesn't matter to Dad – he's already passed on." I didn't realize how much it mattered to me. In my heart I said goodbye to him today and let my brother know how much it meant to me that he was always there for our Dad.

We motor on to Frankenmuth for dinner. We've been here many times before for family dinners. It's a Bavarian town where a lot of German immigrants settled at the turn of the century. The restaurant serves "family style;" dinner is brought to your table on big platters and you pass them around just as you would at home. Chicken and mashed potatoes, all sorts of vegies and gravy – Delicious!

My cousin Linda and her husband John meet us at the Bavarian Inn for dinner. Linda is my Aunt Katie's daughter; Aunt Katie was my favourite aunt when I was a kid and our family spent tons of happy times with them.

Linda and John have ridden out to Frankenmuth on their Harleys. Linda has a beautiful golden orange Softail. She recently downsized from a Road King – and she's no bigger than I am! John has a fire engine red Ultra Classic – gorgeous bikes!

John shows us pictures of his latest project: building motorcycle rocking horses for little kids. He created them for his grandchildren and now he builds them as a fundraiser for various charitable organizations. The last one he made was auctioned off for $1000! He doesn't want to make them to sell for profit. He says he's happy to have the money go for good causes. What a great guy! We part with big hugs as they put on their rain gear and ride into the liquid sunshine.

DAY 52: August 22
Mom's House - Rest Day

It feels good to have a rest day – no plans! Mom and I sleep in and have a lazy morning. We read the paper, work on the crossword puzzle (she's good at crosswords, I am not) and try to figure out which words fit into the little squares. We have several cups of coffee and I catch up on writing in my journal. Ahhh, relaxing!

I need this day to get organized for the next leg of my journey. In two weeks, I have to be back in BC and at work. It's a long haul – 4,000km and it will take me at least ten days of nonstop riding.

I get laundry done (I'm down to my last pair of clean underwear again) and then we go shopping: the hardware store for camping supplies and the grocery store for food. I buy lots of food. I'm not sure how I'm going to fit it all on my bike, but I don't want to have to eat in restaurants all the way across North America.

On the way home, Mom says, "Lets drop by Eileen's – she'd love to see you!" And I would love to see her. Eileen is one of my favorites among my Mom's friends.

I met Eileen several years ago in Hawaii. She and Mom had gone to Hawaii together and rented a place for a month. Mom had phoned me shortly after they got there saying, "Eileen is going to visit friends for a week and I'll be in our place all by myself. I know you have spring break coming up and I bet I can get you a deal on a plane ticket. Why don't you come and keep me company?"

I jumped at the opportunity. I was working my buns off at the time at my day job and also taking classes at Simon Fraser University at night. I desperately needed a break.

I didn't find out until much later that Mom had told Eileen how hard I was working and that Eileen then made arrangements to stay with a friend so I could come to Hawaii for a week to stay with Mom. She did it just for me and we had never even met! What a sweetheart – the two of them planned the whole thing and then presented it to me as if I was doing them a favour!

Eileen was the same as I remembered her – warm and funny and sharp as a tack. "It's quite an adventure you're on!" she said as I hugged her. Mom wanted me to tell her the story of my lost wallet so I did and she laughed and laughed. "That would make a good movie!" she said. We debated whether Meryl Streep or Goldie Hawn should play the lead role and decided on Goldie. We could just imagine her dressed in short baby doll pajamas hugging the tall handsome and somewhat shocked police officer in the motel parking lot at 3:00am!

My brother John phoned me on my cell while Mom and I were visiting Eileen. "How about if Nancy and I take you and Mom out for dinner?" he asked. "I thought you and Nancy had church tonight?" I said. "That's what's nice about being Christian," he replied. "God will forgive us." Mom and I quickly went back to her house after we finished our visit with Eileen, tossed the groceries in the fridge, and met John and Nancy at a neighbourhood restaurant.

John is so thoughtful and so is his wife Nancy. They just wanted a chance to say goodbye before I leave tomorrow. It will probably be at least another year (if not longer) before I see them again. I'm lucky to have such a wonderful family!

DAY 53: August 23
Brighton to
Wilderness State Park,
Mackinaw, Michigan

It's a pack up and move down the road day. Hard to say goodbye to my Mom – I love her so much! While I organize my gear, Mom reads the paper and checks our answers for the crossword puzzle we did yesterday. Hooray! We only missed one word and that was simply because we spelled it wrong. How were we supposed to know how to spell Aikido, an Oriental type of self-defense?

My Mom leads me out to the highway with her car. "Why?" you ask. Because in order to get onto Hwy 23, I have to go through two "circles of death" (as my sister calls them) that are linked together. It's a super bad spot and there's been too many accidents there; they are thinking of totally rebuilding the traffic circles.

Traffic is always heavy in that area.

I follow Mom into the insane circles and onto the highway. She gives me a big wave when she takes her exit and I wave back. I wish I lived closer . . . I wish I got to see her more often. I'm very grateful my brother and my sister are there for her. "You were always the independent one, Mary Jane," she said to me many moons ago. I guess I am. I like being with other people, especially my family, but I also like doing stuff on my own.

I thought this part of the trip would be a bit of a grind (crossing the prairies again) and a little sad (I have to go back to work and reality) but actually I just feel like it's a continuation of the journey. I'm happy to be on Ruby riding down the highway.

My sister suggested that I camp the first night at Wilderness State Park in Mackinaw. My brother and his family have stayed there too, and they seconded my sister's recommendation. It's a little off the beaten path but, my, oh my, what a beautiful park! Its right on Lake Michigan and my campsite is beach side.

Sandy, sandy, sandy! Long sandy beach just a few steps from my tent. I hop off my bike and enjoy sitting on the beach wriggling my toes in the sand. I sit for a long time, listening to the waves, watching them roll in, finding different interesting rocks and absorbing the sun slowly sinking into the water. So peaceful. I'm in no hurry – watching the sunset is more important than setting up my tent in the fading light. (I've done it in the dark many times before – it's not going to be a problem!)

DAY 54: August 24
Mackinaw to Marquette, Michigan

Woke up early to a beautiful sunrise. Sat on the beach and watched the colours change from dark purple to red to pinky orange to golden. Supremely, incredibly, gorgeous!

I thought about packing up and getting an early start on the day but decided, "No rush," and went back to bed for a few hours. Mistake! When I woke up again the sky was dark gray and cloudy.

And then the rain hit; a hard rain with lots of thunder and lightning. I thought, "Its OK; storms in this part of the country are often intense but pass over quickly. I'll just wait it out."

My neighbour from the campsite next door came over and introduced herself; she invited me into their totally covered picnic table dining area for coffee. Her name was Kathy and her husband was John and they had a friendly Irish setter named Otis.

Well, it rained and it rained and it rained more! Lightning arched across the sky, and thunder rumbled as the heavens opened and water poured out. This storm was not going to blow over quickly!

It was all good. John and Kathy were super people to chat with. They live in Grand Rapids which is on the west side of Michigan. They have three grown up boys and Kathy chuckled, "I even have a male dog!" I remarked that she was outnumbered and John laughed and said, "Yes, but we all know who is the boss!"

We sat and talked all morning and into the afternoon. Sometimes the rain would lighten up a bit as a teaser and then it would pour again. The road in front of our campsites was flooded with a foot of water! Thank goodness I had set up my tent on slightly high ground. The water was pooling and streaming everywhere!

Finally the rain stopped. "I'm going to take advantage of this lull to try to pack up my soggy tent," I told John and Kathy, "and then if you don't mind, I'll come back and have another coffee with you."

It's funny, but the conversation was even more relaxed after I packed up. Maybe it was me (I knew I'd be able to make some mileage today) or maybe it was them. I think it was more them than me. While I was there during the rain, I don't think they got it that I really liked them. Yes, I know they invited me over, but I really had no other choice except sitting in my tiny tent. When I had coffee with them after the rain stopped, it was because I chose to – I could've just left at that point, but I didn't because I was enjoying our conversation. I think they understood that I thought they were really neat people who had interesting ideas to share. Big hugs between us when we parted ways.

Over the mighty Mackinaw Bridge again and into Michigan's Upper Peninsula! I'm heading for Marquette, which is where I went to university in the early 1970's. I want to see Lake Superior again and Presque Isle and Sugarloaf Mountain. I had some life changing experiences in those places. Marquette is where I left from when I first hitchhiked out to B.C. and, unbeknownst to me at the time, I never returned to live in Michigan again.

DAY 55: August 25
Marquette, Michigan

Last night I was trying to find the Marquette County campground. As usual, I got lost. I pulled over into a wide spot in the road to check my map and a guy pulls up next to me on a bike. "Are you lost?" he says.

Anyway, we got to talking, and we just kind of instantly hit it off. Before I realized it, 20 minutes had flown by with us chatting by the side of the road. So I did something I don't ever normally do - "If you're not busy tomorrow, do you mind giving me a tour of Marquette?" I asked. He looked surprised, then said "Sure." He gave me his phone number, guided me to the campground, waved goodbye and rode off.

Once again, I have a stunning campsite. I'm in the tenting area on the bank of a small lake. Got here just in time to watch the sunset and get my tent up before dark. As I'm lying in my tent, I start thinking that I would really like to be able to spend a whole day revisiting my old haunts in Marquette, not just tomorrow morning and then hitting the road. I calculate the kilometers and the number of days before I have to return to work. I figure I can spend a full day in Marquette, camp here again tomorrow and still get back to Vancouver by Labour Day. Ahh, that thought feels good as I fall asleep.

Wake up to a gorgeous sunny day. I phone my new friend, Wayne, and let him know I'm going to stay an extra night and there's no rush, so how about if we meet at 1:00? He agrees.

OK, here's a description of Wayne and what I learned about him in the brief talk we had on the side of the road. He rides a 2008 Yamaha V Star, in pristine condition. (What a girl I am; I start by describing the bike!) He's tall, in good shape, about my age, with the usual biker beard. His eyes are blue, almost turquoise, the colour of a glacier fed lake. He has a house and property just down the road that he's been working on for several decades. Married for 27 years and just split up with his wife a few months ago. Super into meditation and Tao Te Ching. He's nice, very nice, which is why I decided to be bold enough to ask him to take me on a tour.

Wayne comes to my campsite at 1:00 and asks where I'd like to go first. I say, "Little Presque Isle." It's one of my favourite places. He decides his jacket is too warm and asks if it's OK if we stop by his place on the way so he can pick up a lighter jacket. We do, and he gives me a tour of the property. It's quite beautiful.

There's a huge pond in his back yard and lots of grass and gardens. It's very well kept up. Next to the pond is an old stone bridge. Wayne explains that the original highway went through his place and that Henry Ford had a "Boys Club" over the bridge and up the road. I can just imagine the Model T Fords driving over that stone bridge, the old boys drinking and smoking cigars.

We head out to Little Presque Isle. It's a short way up the road from Wayne's place. Little Presque is just like I remembered it; it hasn't changed in forty years – still a gravel road and small parking lot, lots of trees and hardly any people. We walk way, way, way down the beach. The sand is all pinky red as well as the rocks. It's a special kind of sandstone that's only on the south side of Lake Superior. I remember it well – and the Mother Superior.

There's something very special about Lake Superior. She's so big you can't see the other side and much deeper than any of the other Great Lakes, a huge body of water with a personality all her own. Lying on the warm red sand with my head against an old beach log, feeling smooth rocks with my fingertips, I listen to the waves brush the shore.

And Wayne and I talk . . . all of it related to spirituality. He's majorly into the Tao Te Ching, which translates as "The Book of the Way." Tao (pronounced Dow) is an Eastern religion anciently related to Buddhism. Lao-tze is the author of the Tao Te Ching and he lived in 500 BC and was a contemporary of Confucius. I know very little about Tao and, since I'm curious, I ask lots of questions. Wayne willingly explains. He's been meditating, studying, and doing yoga for forty years.

We talk about the relationship between all religions, how there's only one God but so many different pathways to him. How most religions teach that their path is the only one and the dissension this causes between people. Everyone's goal is to reach a "Christ consciousness" but that state of being is called many different names depending on your religion. Christians appear to only practice their spirituality on Sundays whereas in most Eastern religions, spirituality is an everyday way of life.

A lot of what we're talking about resonates for me with things I learned in the Czech Republic about Comenius in "The Labyrinth of the World and the Paradise of the Heart." And also with the things I learned about ancient Shamanism in Siberia from a course I took at SFU. It seems to be all connected.

We're hungry and Wayne suggests we ride into downtown Marquette to his favourite Mexican restaurant which has a patio overlooking the harbor. I'm falling in love with Marquette again and I say so to Wayne. "Oh darn," he responds, "I was trying to get you to fall in love with me!" I laugh and tell him he's "a sweetheart" because I really don't know how to handle that comment. He gets kind of quiet after that. Maybe he said more than he meant to. We order beer and really delicious fish tacos. It's beautiful sitting on the patio with a gorgeous view of the sailboats going in and out of the harbor and a tall ship moored at the dock.

The conversation turns to emotions. Wayne says one of his challenges is to control his emotions. I disagree and I tell him that I think we need to accept our emotions: that we are spiritual beings having a physical experience and that emotions are part of the experience. He says, "OK, let me explain it differently – I don't want my emotions to control my decisions." That's a statement I can agree with.

But we disagree on how emotions fit into the trinity of mind, spirit, and body. Wayne feels emotions are tied to mind but I don't think so – I think they are in the center influencing all three. We agree to disagree.

After dinner, we go for a walk in downtown Marquette; I love downtown Marquette. Its full of buildings that are over 100 years old and made out of big blocks of that beautiful local pink sandstone. The stores are all closed now; Marquette rolls up the sidewalks at 5 pm, but that's OK. I didn't want to buy anything anyway, just look in the store windows and feel the ambiance. It feels pretty much the same as it did when I lived here in the 70's; it's a good feeling.

We hop back on the bikes and ride out to Big Presque Isle. It's kind of like Stanley Park in Vancouver but smaller. It's a popular spot to watch the sunset and we park the bikes and sit on some stumps on a cliff high above the water.

We're quiet and suddenly Wayne touches my arm and points to the ground. There's a huge Gartner snake slithering, sliding close to our feet. "She's beautiful," he says quietly, "I don't know why she's not scared of us." I can see the snake's sides go in and out as she breathes. It's like she's searching for something – she slowly moves this way and that, pausing often, then turns and slithers back across the same ground she's covered. Her head moves back and forth, looking here and there, and her tongue constantly flicks in and out.

I slowly place my hand flat on the ground. She slides over and flicks her tongue several times on my fingertips. It feels like light kisses. As she slithers away, I gently touch her skin. She's not startled or scared; she just goes on her way. Wow! I wonder what she came here to tell me?

We go back to Wayne's house. He wants to look up my birth signs according to Chinese astrology.

My year is 1953 – The year of the Water Snake. Wayne prints an information sheet about the year of the Snake. It says, *Those born under the sign of the Water Snake are charming and popular but not noisy or outspoken. They are determined to follow through on any-*

thing they undertake. They make decisions quickly and firmly. They are deep thinkers and very philosophical. They rely heavily on first impressions and their own feelings rather than facts or the opinions of others. They seem to have a sixth sense in this way.

Like ordinary astrology, I think Chinese astrology is a general indicator. You can't run your life by it. And I believe that every human being is created by "Nature and Nurture" – you are born with certain attributes and tendencies that are either brought forth or lay dormant depending on your experiences.

Wayne and I sit and drink tea and talk more about astrology and Tao and our various life experiences. He spent the first twenty years of his career being a carpenter, then got his masters in Environmental Engineering and worked for the government for twenty years. He retired a few years ago and is enjoying having more time to garden, work on his house, meditate and ride his motorcycles. (Yes, he has two bikes; the Yamaha V Star and an amazing retro bike that he built by hand. Her name is Dragon.)

He tempts me with if I could spend one more day, we could ride and explore more places, he'd cook for me and we could watch the stars from his outdoor hot tub. (Oh, the things men will say when they want to go to bed with you!) I decline graciously and he accepts my answer respectfully. I like him and maybe if I knew him better I'd let him park his boots under my bed, but I don't know him better and there's not enough time. I didn't undertake this trip with the intention of fucking my way across the continent and back and I'm certainly not going to start now.

Wayne rides me to my campsite (I love it when men walk me home) and we say goodbye. He gives me a kiss (Wow! What a kiss!) and I have to pull back and say "Stop." I know if I don't, my resolve to sleep in my little tent by myself will melt away (Maybe? Maybe not? Whatever – I've already decided – No.)

I sit in front of my tent for a while looking out at the lake. Should I change my mind and stay for another day? I can't. It is what it is: a chance meeting of two kindred spirits. As much as we so easily intermesh with each other, there's no more time and thousands of kilometers between the places we each call home.

Treasure the moment, Mary Jane. Be happy with that.

DAY 56: August 26
Marquette, Michigan to
Grand Rapids, Minnesota

Today is a mileage-making day. I want to get some kilometers behind me. My goal is get to Grand Rapids, Minnesota. Its 500 km. That's more kilometers than I like to do, but there's a cheap motel that I stayed at on the way east; I can do more miles when I don't have to set up camp. And I can sleep in a bed! And have a hot shower! And maybe even buy a can of beer! Sounds like good incentives to put in the extra miles.

The morning is cloudy and I pack up my tent quickly before the rain hits. It's just light rain and I'm wearing rain gear; it's all good. I hate it when it rains so hard that I can't see. That doesn't happen today but on the days when it does, I don't like it. My visibility becomes extremely limited and I just try to stay in my lane with the rubber side down until I can find a restaurant to take shelter in. Today it's just on and off light showers.

Riding gives me lots of time to think. I mean, I'm watching the road for potholes and road snakes, I'm watching other drivers as they pass me or I pass them, I'm watching the scenery as the trees and lakes and small towns pass by; but besides all that, riding gives me time to just think all sorts of things over in my head and heart.

Before I left Wayne's house last night, he asked me if I had room in my saddlebags for a book. I hesitated because Ruby is packed to the max (and then some! I have to sit on my bags to get the zippers done up.) I answered, "Yes. If it's a small book." He gave me a pocket edition of the Tao Te Ching. It was wrapped in bookstore wrapping paper. He said he'd bought it as a gift a long time ago, knowing he'd want to pass its knowledge on to someone but not knowing whom. I guess it was waiting for me. Funny how life works sometimes.

Tao Te Ching means *The Book of the Way and How It Manifests Itself in the World.* I've only read the forward so far and I think about what it says while I'm riding.

Lao-tzu is the author and his name translates to "the old boy." I like that – to me it indicates he was a wise man with a childlike innocence. You know like when you see a baby who has those eyes that make you think, "Here in lies an old soul." Anyway, there's very little written about Lao-tzu in history. The forward says, *Like an Iroquois woodsman, he left no traces; all he left us is his book.* I like that too.

The forward talks about the apparent paradox of opposites. It's a difficult concept for me to get my head around: I can feel it, but I can't logically understand it. It's the concept of yin and yang – opposites but at the same time, a whole.

I never noticed before that the yin and yang symbols contain each other's light and darkness. In the dark part, there is a circle of light; in the light part there is a circle of dark. Interesting. There is yin within the yang and yang within the yin.

The forward talks about the paradox of "doing not-doing" or "Wei wu wei." I remember that feeling a long time ago when I was kayaking down a river. I was paddling, yet it was effortless. The current of the river was carrying me but it was more than that. There was a synergy between my paddling and the river's current that blended the two together so that the energies of both were indiscernible from each other. I remember thinking, "This is how life should be."

Quote from the forward of the Tao Te Ching: *Less and less do you need to force things, until finally you arrive at non-action. When nothing is done, nothing is left undone.* I wonder if this is the essence of what Kat means when she talks about how the world needs a paradigm shift: a shift from seeing things as separate, to seeing them as part of a greater whole. It's difficult for me to put it into words; I do better at just feeling it, especially when I look up into the darkness of the night sky ablaze with tiny pinpoints of light.

It's been a good day. Lots to think about, good roads, some sun, some rain and I'm tired and happy when I get to my hotel in Grand

Rapids. The owner remembers me and gives me the same room. Almost feels like home. I go to the liquor store across the street, buy myself a can of beer and drink it while I eat tuna and crackers and cheese. (If you count beer as a vegetable, that's all four food groups!) Have a shower (hot, hot, hot!) and hit the bed (very, very comfy.) Zzzzzzzzzz...

DAY 57: August 27
Grand Rapids, Minnesota to
Devils Lake, North Dakota

Ahhhh! It felt so good to sleep in a real bed again. I love my little tent, but a bed is way more comfortable.

The weather network forecasted rain for Grand Rapids today but when I wake up its only cloudy. Good! I pack up all the gear I spread out in the hotel room to dry last night and hit the road.

Before I leave Grand Rapids, I Google North Dakota State Parks. I stayed at Turtle River State Park on my way east but I heard people say good things about Graham Island State Park near Devils Lake. I decide to head there on my old friend Hwy #2.

I like Hwy #2. I rode it most of the way east from Glacier National Park to Michigan. It's a well-paved secondary road with not much traffic. The semi-trucks and the mileage makers are on the toll expressway just south of here.

About 200 km down the road the rain hits. Remember the hard rain that I hate and described yesterday? That's what this is. I can hardly see; I can't even drive defensively – I'm just trying to stay in my lane and hope the other vehicles stay in theirs. Yuk!

Thankfully there's a town a few kilometers down the road. I pull into the parking lot of the A&W. I go inside and sit at a table for four so I can spread out my soaking wet gear on all the chairs to dry. It is bucketing outside and my riding gear is dripping puddles onto the floor. It's a good place to hang out; they have Wi-Fi and their burgers are organic. I check my emails and Facebook. There's a nice message from Wayne which makes me smile.

The rain goes on for a couple hours. That's OK; I'm toasty warm and dry in the A&W. When it finally stops raining, I put on more warm layers including my heated vest and hit the road. A sign in town says the temperature is 58 degrees. Brrrr!

Graham Island is 22 miles outside of Devils Lake. My map neglected to tell me the road is under construction. It's paved (sort of) but there are huge strips of missing asphalt where the pavement starts and stops. I hit the first one at 40 kmph, and bottom out my suspension. Shit! I hope I didn't bend my front rim! I slow to a crawl for every missing strip of asphalt after that. Thank goodness they're marked.

I start to think I've gone too far on this horrid road. My odometer is in km, so I have to convert, but I figure I've gone 30 miles and the park turn off is supposed to be at 22. The sun is setting and I definitely do not want to be on this road lost in the dark.

I phone the park office. "Oh," the ranger says, "They probably took the sign down again because it was in the way of the construction. If you turn around, our road will be five miles past the first bridge."

I turn around and head back up the road, slowing for the missing asphalt strips and being careful on the gravel. The sun has set and the bugs are so thick that I have to pull my visor down and keep my lips shut to keep the nasty critters out of my eyes and mouth.

Finally find the turnoff for the park; there's a small sign leaning against some sand bags from this direction but nothing from the direction I first came. There's no way I could have known where it was – Jeeeez!

It's another five miles down the road to the campground. The bugs are horrific and there are so many plastered on my windshield I can hardly see through it. At least my visor is keeping them out of my eyes.

Finally pull up in front of the ranger's office. He comes out and says, "You riding solo?" "Yeah, I am," I reply. "Good to see a woman on a bike!" he exclaims emphatically. Just to hear him say that cheers me up – it's been a bit of a rough day, between torrential rain and billions of bugs.

My campsite is beautiful: grassy, treed, with a view of the lake. There's a strong breeze which blows the bugs away. Hooray! I set up my tent in the dark, and eat my dinner by candlelight. The day was a little tough, but it all worked out. Thanks God.

DAY 58: August 28
Devils Lake to Williston, North Dakota

Tolston, the Park Ranger, comes over to chat with me this morning. Of course he used to ride a bike! He tells me about some amazing trips that he and his wife went on. They rode two up and pulled one of those tiny little pop-up campers that are made for motorcycles. Fun! They traveled all over the U.S. and Canada. Now he's had both knees replaced and his wife just recently had a hip replacement. He says his buddies keep bugging him to ride again but he feels his riding days are over. He doesn't regret not riding anymore – he's happy with his life.

It's so nice to pack up a dry tent and way easier. Lighter too, not carrying all that water. It's a super sunny day and it's hot already this morning. Weird; yesterday I was freezing and today I'm going to be boiling!

I meet a couple of bikers at a gas station down the road, a man and a woman and their son. The woman is super chatty – you know, the kind of person who just keeps talking and talking and you can't get a word in edgewise? It's more than a little annoying. She's very bubbly and happy, which is nice, but she never stops talking – not even to breathe! I just want to get out of there.

While his wife is in the store, the man hands me a book and says, "My wife wants you to have this." I look at the title, *Hope for the Highway*, put out by the Christian Motorcycle Association. Oh, OK, I get it, they're Bikers for Jesus.

I take the book and say thanks and ride off, not intending to read it. But later, when I take a break to get something to eat, I pull it out. It's actually quite interesting. It's written for motorcyclists and on the first page in bold print it says, *FREEDOM! No other word describes what it feels like to drive straight toward the horizon.*

Alright, so whoever wrote this book gets what riding motorcycles is all about. The book has stories written by bikers who found Jesus, which are intermeshed with an easy to understand summary of the Old Testament and the entire New Testament. In spite of myself, I enjoy reading it.

Reading the Bikers for Jesus book makes me think about a lot of things again while I'm riding; I studied the writings of Comenius when I was in Prague last year and he made an impact on me. Centuries ago, he talked about how all Christian religions pray to the same God. He tried to stop the incessant fighting in Europe between Catholics and Protestants.

Comenius had an image of Jesus in some of his writings that I prefer over the standard Christian religious image of Jesus dying on the cross. (That image always gives me a not-so-good feeling – like its saying that all humans are evil sinners.) Comenius drew an image of JC standing with his arms outstretched and welcoming – like he was just waiting to give you a hug! And his heart shone through his white robe a glowing pinkish red magenta colour with a flame shining golden within. Beautiful . . . I like that image of Jesus. It reminds me of a kid's song, *This little light of mine, I'm gonna let it shine . . .*

As I ride, I hum my song and think about all my positive experiences with Christianity: the old, old churches in Europe, not the fancy ones but the simple stone and timber ones in the small villages. My very favourite one had no walls and no roof; it was simply a stone alter on top of a hillside with a 360-degree view of the countryside. The worshippers had sat on half split log benches – the wooden remnants were still there. What did Thoreau write once? *I believe in God; I spell his name N-a-t-u-r-e.*

It occurs to me that I am experiencing many kinds of spirituality on this road trip: "Creating a Caring Community" with Kat and her friends, "Human Design" with Michel and Claudia, "Tao Te Ching" with Wayne and now "Riding for the Son" with the Christian couple. I'm grateful; I figure I have lots to learn about spirituality.

I'm heading for Lewis and Clark State Park. Its 500 km from Graham Island (another long day) but I find a short cut that will save me 80 km. I saw it on the map this morning but I wasn't sure whether or not it was paved. Hooray, it is!

Except I get lost; now that's nothing new, is it? Not very lost, just a little. I saw the sign that said "Lewis and Clark State Park 3 km." but what I didn't see was the arrow underneath indicating I should turn left and then go 3 km. Once again, I am sitting on the side of the road with my map out. And once again, a vehicle stops and asks if I'm lost.

But this time it's different: I haven't seen a vehicle on this road for over an hour and this particular vehicle comes from a long side road trailing a cloud of dust. When they stop, my mind goes to a conversation I had with Kathy during the monsoon I sat out in her and John's covered picnic table area drinking coffee in Michigan. "Aren't you afraid traveling by yourself?" she had asked. "No," I replied. "Everyone I meet is super nice and really helpful." "But what if you were in the middle of nowhere and a truck full of big scary men pulled up beside you?" I had laughed, "That sounds like the movie Deliverance," I said, "not like reality."

But here I am in the middle of nowhere and the van that has stopped to ask if I'm lost is full of big burly oilmen who must have just finished a shift on the rigs. Their faces are greasy and black as well as their clothes and hands. They look like pictures I've seen of Appalachian coal miners and Deliverance immediately comes to mind. "I'm looking for Lewis and Clark State Park," I say in my bravest voice, "but I think I passed it." "Yeah," the driver answers. "It's 5 miles back the way you came from." I thank him, and several of the men in the back of the van smile and wave as they drive off. I am grateful that the world of reality is not anything like the movies.

The 3-km ride into the park is beautiful; these are the Dakota Badlands and the road winds around bluffs and escarpments toward Lake Sakakawea. The lake is named after the female Indian guide who led Meriwether Lewis all the way to the west coast. Lewis and Clark felt that if they had a female guide, the tribes they met along the way would see them as friendly – and they were right! Sakakawea was beautiful and smart and if the relationship between her and Meriwether was romantic, history doesn't acknowledge it. (But come on now, it doesn't take much imagination...)

The park rangers are two young girls in their twenties. They lead me in their truck to my campsite because I confess to them that it's been a long day and I'm directionally challenged. Besides, I would like a bundle of firewood and there's no way I can carry it on my bike. They're really sweet young women. One of them is going back to school in the fall to start her Masters and the other one is applying to the Air Force to become a pilot. Being a park ranger is a seasonal job for them and they are both a long way from their homes in Michigan and Pennsylvania. They have never been out of their home states before. They both admit that they were scared to come all the way out to North Dakota to be park rangers, but that once they got here it was fine. I agree – I tell them I was afraid before I started on this trip too.

My campsite is amazing. I must be blessed to get so many sites overlooking the ocean or a lake! Its right on Lake Sakakawea with the bluffs in the distance across the water ... and there is no one else here! I mean there are people within sight way over in the Winnebago area, but I have a whole acre of tenting sites all to myself.

And I get to set up my tent in the daylight! Now that is a novelty. And make my dinner without using a flashlight. And watch the sunset and even build a campfire.

Ahhh, man – Life is so good!

DAY 59: August 29
Williston, North Dakota
to Glasgow, Montana

It was so relaxing last night, sitting by the campfire, watching the flames do their dance. This is a special place. The beach is down a little trail right in front of my tent; when I wake up in the morning I go for a walk.

It's not a sandy beach; instead it's full of interesting rocks. All different colours – red ones that have no weight to them like porous bricks, white and yellow agate looking ones, dark black coal like ones and speckled black and white salt and peppery ones. Some smooth, some sharp, some broken, some whole . . . all different . . . like people or snowflakes.

I slowly eat my breakfast and pack up my camping gear. It's hard to leave such a beautiful peaceful place. Before I head out, I remember that Ruby needs her oil topped up and since Williston is a bigger sized city maybe there is a Harley Davidson dealer. What Ruby really requires is an oil change, not just a top up.

I ride into Williston, stop to get gas and ask if there's a HD dealer in town. There is! The girl in the gas station tells me it just opened a couple months ago and she gives me great directions. Such good directions in fact, that even though there are lots of turns, I don't get lost. Yay!

The HD dealership is called "Black Magic" and it's an incredibly enormous store. I go into the service department hoping they can fit Ruby in for an oil change. The guy at the desk ignores me; he's doing something on his computer. I wait. A girl comes out from the back and says, "Do you need help?" I answer, "Yes," and explain that I'm traveling and that my bike is desperately in need of an oil change.

Her name is Cameo. She says, "I'll check with the mechanics," and disappears through the door again. I'm keeping my fingers crossed.

Cameo comes back and tells me the mechanics will do an oil change for me right now. I thank her profusely and ride my bike into the shop. Cameo shows me to a waiting area in the store with fancy leather couches where I can sit and relax.

After about half an hour, a service manager comes and introduces himself as Patrick. "I want to show you something on your bike," he says. "Come into the shop with me." My heart sinks.

As we walk towards the shop, Patrick explains, "I'm not trying to up-sell you. The mechanic noticed that you have hardly any tread left on your rear tire. It's definitely hydroplane material if you hit rain. How far do you have to get home?" he asks. "About 2,000 km," I answer. He shakes his head. "That tire won't make it that far."

Patrick introduces me to Cory, the mechanic working on my bike, and shows me my tire. It's almost bald along the centerline. All the extra weight in gear that I'm carrying has caused it to wear out quicker than normal.

I ask Patrick if they have my tire in stock and he checks with Cameo. Yes, they do! "Please install it," I say.

I feel very fortunate: fortunate that there's a HD dealer in Williston, fortunate that Cameo fit me in for an oil change, fortunate that Cory noticed my rear tire, fortunate that they had a replacement tire in stock. I am grateful. Thank you universe. The alternative could have been topping up Ruby's oil and having a blowout down the road.

But now its 4:00. I certainly am not going to rack up very many kilometers today and I'm not even sure where I'm going to sleep.

Hit the road, heading west and ride about 200 km. Stop for gas and sit on my bike in the parking lot drinking a container of milk and eating a granola bar. There's about two hours of daylight left and I'm thinking I better figure out where I'm going to spend the night.

A county sheriff pulls up next to me and says, "Hello." Does he ride? Of course he does. We talk about bikes and roads and traveling. I ask him if there are any campgrounds an hour ride west of here. He tells me that New Glasgow is about 70 miles and that it has several campgrounds just off the highway. Good; now I know where I'm going to sleep tonight.

I can't find the campground that the county sheriff recommended but I see a sign for another one. I head up a gravel road and turn into the driveway. It looks OK from outside the office. A woman comes out through the office door and lets me know it's only $15 for a tent site. Deal! I pay up and drive past the office to pick out a spot.

That's when I realize that I'm in a place that could be used as a location for a '"Trailer Park'" movie. There are dilapidated trailers, caved in sheds and just plain junk everywhere. It is a campground, sort of, but it's also a place where oilfield workers house their families in tin trailers while they go to work.

I keep telling myself that it's just for one night, that it's cheap and that I will survive.

A couple little boys come by riding their bikes and stop to admire Ruby. We talk for a bit and of course they have to show off to me how they can get "big air" going fast over the bumps in the road. They ask me if I can do a wheelie and when I say "No" they ride off unimpressed.

Two little girls come over to admire my teddy bear. The older one is Emily (she tells me proudly that she is 8) and she has her 3-year-old sister Abby in tow. She's obviously taking care of her – there are no adults anywhere to be seen. Emily asks if I need help putting up my tent. I really don't, but I know she'd like to help, so I say "Yes" and she and Abby and I try to get my tent set up. I'm having trouble with it because I'm not used to doing it with two little kids; we talk about how when something doesn't work at first, you just try again. Emily is a sweetheart and very kind to Abby.

The two boys on bicycles come back and one of them, Austin, tells Emily, "Mom wants you to bring Abby home now." Austin is their big brother and the other boy is his cousin. I get that they live in a couple of the ramshackle trailers.

I like Austin; he's an OK kid. He notices that I have a hammock (yeah, the boys are looking through all my camping gear.) It occurs to me that maybe they're figuring out what they would like to steal, but I push the thought aside. They're just curious kids.

Austin wants to sleep in my hammock. I tell him, "It's alright with me but you have to ask your Mom." Excitedly he races home only to return moments later with a very sad face; "Mom says you're a stranger and she says No." I tell Austin that his mom is smart and that she's right. He's so bummed out that I tell him to go ask his Mom if he can borrow my hammock and I'll help him set it up by his trailer. (I realize, of course, that if Austin's Mom says yes, I may never see my hammock again.)

Austin comes back on his bicycle singing, "It's a wonderful wonderful day!" His Mom said, "Yes." He's so excited he's kind of jumping all over the place.

He leads me over to his trailer carrying the hammock and I bring the rope. Again, there are no adults to be seen, although I can hear a lot of yelling going on in the trailer. The yard is a total disaster area. There's junk everywhere: old pails and car parts and broken toys and a half falling down swing set and a couple dogs running around barking. Holy shit, what have I gotten myself into?

Austin helps me tie the hammock between two trees. He is babbling on about how he's going to put his blanket in it and lay there and look at the stars and read his book with a flashlight. He's very, very, very happy. I'm kind of getting the impression that his life is not that great; I'm glad that a least maybe I brought something positive into it. He really is a good kid with a big heart and an even bigger imagination,

I head back to my campsite (nope, I never did meet Austin's parents and I don't think I want to), make myself some dinner and read for a bit before I go to bed. I lock down my saddlebags and put anything I can't afford to have stolen in my tent with me.

I really do think Austin and Emily and Abby and their cousins are nice kids, but I also think it's very weird that the only adult I've seen was the lady outside the front office. This is one strange place . . .

DAY 60: August 30
Glasgow to Shelby, Montana

When I wake up in the morning, it's windier than heck. I don't bother to try to make breakfast; I'll never be able to get my stove lit in this wind and besides, I just want to pack up and get out of here.

I load my camping gear onto Ruby and then, when everything is tied down and ready to go, I walk over to Austin's trailer. I'm prepared for a quick exit if things go awry.

Austin is in the backyard. He's playing catch with Emily with a stuffed animal through her bedroom window. She's inside standing on her bed and they're both laughing. I call out, "Good Morning!" and they both excitedly say "Hi!"

Austin comes over to where I'm taking down the hammock and helps me. He goes on and on enthusiastically about how much fun he had and how many stars there were and how he wasn't scared even though it was really dark. I tell him that he has a great imagination and that I bet he could write a super good story about sleeping in the hammock. He pauses and looks right at me, "Really? You really think so?" It's like nobody has ever told him he's good at anything before.

I reiterate that I think he's smart and creative and maybe in school this year he could write down some of the stories he creates in his head. "Oh, we don't get to do that in school," he says. That's disappointing...

I shake Austin's hand and tell him it was a pleasure to meet him. In a very grown up manner he says, "I liked meeting you too." Emily yells from the bedroom window, "Are you leaving?"

I walk over to her bedroom window, say goodbye and shake her hand. "Will you come back?" she asks. "Yeah, will you come back?" Austin echoes. "Maybe next summer," I reply. "I live a long way away." "Where?" asks Austin. "I live in Canada," I explain. "In a city called Vancouver. It's above Washington State. When you go back to school, you can look on a map or a globe. You'll see it." "Vancouver," Austin repeats slowly. I know he'll look. He's a curious kid. "Bye!" both he and Emily call out and wave as I walk back to Ruby.

In all those interactions with them I never saw or heard an adult – except the yelling in the trailer last night. In fact, I haven't seen any adults all morning either. It's like these kids are raising themselves. I'm glad I met them. They're good kids; I hope they can stay that way.

I head back out on my old friend Hwy #2. There's a peaceful feeling about riding on the prairies. The road goes straight toward the horizon. It feels good to just keep riding right into that horizon. Like you know where you're going and your path is laid out for you.

And the prairies are not really flat or boring; there are farms with the houses surrounded by trees to break the wind. And the hay has just been cut; the big round bales are sitting in the fields waiting to be picked up. There are little hills and creeks and marshy ponds and cows. The train tracks run next to the highway and intermittently a train goes by in one direction or the other.

I'm hungry so I stop in a small town at a café. The place is full of local ranchers talking about the price of hay and how many acres they have left to cut. They're wearing dusty cowboy hats and boots. The waitress calls me "Hon," every time she asks me if I need anything. She's got the same slow drawl as the ranchers. It's a welcoming place.

On the road again, I'm hoping to get to Glacier Park tonight. But I'm tired today and I end up stopping often. I slept all right last night, despite the strange accommodation. I think it's just tiredness from being on the road so many days in a row.

When I get to Shelby, Montana, I stop for gas. It's about 150 more km to Glacier and I contemplate pushing on, but I know that means it'll be dark when I get there.

Instead I go to the Info Center across the street. The woman there tells me that Shelby has a county campground a few miles off the highway. Great! I like county campgrounds; they're always small, well kept up, and affordable.

And I'm not disappointed! It's a nice little campground with super thick grass to set my tent up on. There are clean washrooms and a few other bikers are camped here too. The bikers are all couples with those cute little pop up tent trailers. They're friendly, but we're all tired so we chat for a little bit and then each do our own thing to get prepared for another riding day tomorrow.

I'm glad I stopped here instead of pushing on. Good night.

DAY 61: August 31
Shelby, Montana to Glacier National Park

Last night at about 2:00am it got super windy – and I mean super windy! If my bike hadn't been pointed into the direction the wind was coming from I think it would have blown over.

Everyone in the campground got out of their tents and trailers to batten down the hatches. (Including me!) People were rolling up their awnings and taking down their tarps to keep them from being ripped to shreds.

My tent is fairly low profile and I was tucked in behind a small fir tree. I wasn't worried as much about the wind as I was concerned about the driving rain that might accompany it. I made sure my tent fly was secure and well tucked in so I could weather any weather. LOL! I swear to God my whole tent would have blown away if I wasn't laying in it. But no rain, thank goodness, just wind...

Everybody was talking about our blustery night over coffee in the morning. The people camping in trailers said they woke up because their beds were shaking! We all managed to survive without any damage.

On my way out of town, I noticed an old stone church with beautiful stained-glass windows and I stopped to take a closer look. I was taking some photos when a man came over from the house next door and introduced himself as Father Tim. I commented on what a beautiful church it was and he asked me if I wanted to go inside. I jumped at the opportunity.

The stained-glass windows were even prettier from the inside with the sunlight shining through them. I asked Father Tim if I could sit for a minute and he said, "By all means, go right ahead."

I sat in the front pew and had a little chat with God. Told him how grateful I was to have the opportunity for this journey and all the amazing people I'd met and all the incredible experiences I'd had. Just wanted to tell Him that I was really really thankful and that I don't know what his purpose is for my life but that I'm willing to let His light shine through me. Kind of a simple prayer, but I had tears running down my face when I finished. I thanked Father Tim, said goodbye and headed west out of Shelby. Glacier National Park is only about 100 km down the road.

Man, am I ever glad I didn't try to push on and do this road last night! Its narrow, with no shoulder and there are frost heaves everywhere.

And cows all over the place, including on the road! The first bull I came to just stood in the middle of my lane, not moving a muscle. I wasn't sure what to do; I stopped and we stared at each other. I didn't want to try to go around him; he might charge me and he's bigger than Ruby. I just stayed real still and gunned the motor loudly. He took off, thank goodness. I must have seen two or three dozen more cows as I slowly rode on.

I was really hungry by the time I got to the East Entrance of Glacier. There's a high-priced tourist resort there that I really didn't want to go to. I had noticed a faded wooden sign that said "Johnson's Café and Cabins 2 miles" so I took the gravel side road and went up a hill.

Turned out to be a gorgeous little place established at the turn of the century and built out of logs. Tons of artifacts inside including coal oil lamps and deer antlers on the walls. The place was like a museum.

Super friendly waitress named Salinas told me the lunch special was homemade soup and corned beef and Swiss on rye. I didn't even look at the menu – I just told her I'd have the special – it sounded good.

And it was! Probably one of the best meals I've had on this trip. Salinas came over to see how I was doing and I said, "Please give my compliments to the chef!" She smiled; I was definitely a happy customer.

When she came back to my table, Salinas asked me if I had room for homemade pie. Oh, I was so tempted, but I told her,

"I can't even finish my soup!" "Well, take it with you," she said. "Then you'll have room for pie." "On my bike?" I queried. She went in the kitchen and got me a to-go container that was actually spill proof enough for my saddlebag. Yes! I ordered strawberry rhubarb pie with vanilla ice cream. Yum!

Salinas and I chatted for awhile; turns out she's a bit of a gypsy. She goes to university (on and off) in Idaho and travels around supporting herself as a waitress. She's majoring in criminology and has done volunteer work with at-risk teens. She says, "They listen to me, I'm not sure why." I tell her it's because they know that she likes them. She agrees and asks me what I do. When I tell her I work with kids who have Autism, she says, "You're a good person too." We exchange big hugs; I wish her well in her journey and she says with a smile, "Safe Ride."

I'm finally in Glacier National Park on the Going to the Sun Road once again. It's as beautiful as it was when I came through in July from the other direction. Home sweet home in the mountains! Tall jagged peaks, deep valleys, wide lakes, rushing rivers, cascading waterfalls – it's a gorgeous ride. Even though it's a gray cloudy day, it's not raining and it sure is pretty. Ruby and I are happy.

I'm heading for a campground that's right on a lake. When Razz, Wendy, Donna and I were here in July we wanted to stay at this particular campground but it was full. I'm hoping there'll be an empty site today.

Shit! The campground sign says "Full" but I pull in any way to check and see. There are no empty sites, but there is an area for hikers and bikers to camp. A sign says "For campers with no motorized vehicles."

Hmmmmm . . . I know Ruby has a motor but I really want to camp here. How can I manage this?

I go chat with a couple of young guys from New York State and explain my dilemma. I think they feel bad because they pulled in just before me and took the last available site. They agree to let me park Ruby in their site and then I can just walk over and camp in the hiker/biker area. Perfect!

I unload my gear and carry it over. There are two cyclists from Ohio there already, Ken and Lisa. They ask me if I'm a hiker (and I'm not going to lie to them) so I explain the situation, being sure to say that I am more than willing to share my site if a bona fide hiker/biker rolls in. Ken teases me in a serious tone of voice; "My cousin is the Park Ranger and I'm gonna tell him the truth about you." Then he laughs; I had believed him for half a second!

Lisa says she's heading down to the beach and asks if I want to come. For sure! I can always set up my tent later. The lake is calm and the sun comes out as we sit on the rocks, drinking beer and enjoying the view.

Lisa is a talker. But she doesn't mind being interrupted; sometimes we're both talking at the same time. It's kind of like when you're with an old friend and you finish each other's sentences. And we're both on the same page; it's all good.

She's madly in love with Ken; she calls him "my Hero." They've been together twelve years and he's 71 and she's 53. Ken is physically his age; he moves slowly and he talks slowly and he forgets things. It doesn't seem to bother Lisa. In contrast, she is a live wire, joyful, upbeat, a bit crazy, kind of like a seventeen-year-old hippie chick. I think she brings a lot of joy into Ken's life and he brings stableness and security into hers.

We talk about religion (she was raised Baptist), and how Buddha and Jesus were both equally amazing teachers. We discuss how life is a combination of destiny and choices and how each of our paths is fluid – your destiny changes based on the choices you make. It feels so good to chat with Lisa. Like I said, we're both on the same page.

Ken comes down and joins us at the beach. He falls asleep in the warm sunshine and he snores. Lisa and I laugh; it's kind of like lying on the rocks with a hibernating bear.

When the sun starts to set, Lisa gently wakes Ken, "Sweetheart, wake up and watch the sunset with us. It's gonna be beautiful." The three of us continue our conversation about life and how fortunate we are. Ken says that he figures, "Whatever our Mentality, Creates our Reality." I think those are words of wisdom and I tell him so.

He's right – the way in which we perceive the world has an effect on the experiences that come our way. If we think the world is a scary dangerous place full of evil people, those are exactly the experiences that happen to us. If we believe that people are basically good and wanting to help us on our journey, those are the people that we meet.

I'm not saying it works that way all the time. Sometimes bad shit happens to good people. But most of the time, you get what you give.

I go back to our campsite, set up my tent, eat dinner, and drink whiskey by the campfire with Lisa and Ken. Life is good; thank you Universe.

DAY 62: September 1
Glacier National Park, Montana
to Riders Ranch Motorcycle
Campground in Creston, B.C.

Hang out in the morning with Lisa and Ken drinking coffee and eating breakfast. Like many other spots that I've camped, it's a hard place to leave. I go down to the beach one last time, give my two new friends hugs, and head out of the park.

I'm thinking that if I can get to Toad Rock Campground tonight I could stay for two whole nights. I'm not really sure how far it is – I'll Google it later when I'm somewhere where there is Wi-Fi. It would be nice to stay two nights in the same place.

I go through Whitefish, Montana and head north towards the Canadian border. I'm just outside of town where the speed limit changes from city (45mph) to highway (70mph) so I begin to accelerate. I see a white pickup truck stopped at a stop sign on a gravel side road up ahead on my right. He's at a dead stop; I check his wheels, they're not moving. He looks right at me . . . and then pulls out in front of me making a left turn! Holy Fuck! My brain says calmly, *I'm going to hit him.* It's not a panic thought, it's a logical fact. It seems like everything is happening in slow motion. I jam on both brakes as hard as I can without locking them up and skidding, trying to drop as much speed as possible. I can see his face when he finally sees me. His eyes go wide and his mouth drops open. Thankfully, he has enough sense to hit the accelerator hard and he spins out of my path burning rubber. I scoot around his rear bumper missing him by inches.

Holy Jesus . . . that was so close! My heart is pounding. How could he look right at me and not see me? Was his brain looking for a car and the fact that there was a motorcycle coming just didn't compute until the very last minute? I could tell by his face he didn't do it on purpose. He really did look down the road and not see me even though I was right there. Really really scary.

I haven't had a close call like that this whole trip and now, when I'm almost home, I nearly die!

I stick to the speed limit, carefully watching the cars. I don't want somebody doing something stupid in front of me again. I just want to get home in one piece!

About an hour down the road, a guy in a truck in the oncoming lane pulls a left turn right across my lane onto a gravel side road. No turn signal, nothing. It's not all that close but I have to jam on the brakes. And I know he saw me – he was just being an asshole. I chalk it up to that he has an unhappy life and he's jealous that I'm on a bike and he's not.

Shit! Two close calls in one day. Maybe once I get across the border into Canada I will be safer! At least it's a nice day, not totally sunny, but the sun peeks out from the clouds every now and then, and there's no hint of rain. I cross the border and head west.

By the time I get to Cranbrook, I realize that there is no way I am going to make it to Toad Rock tonight. I remember there's a motorcycle campground close to Creston that I've passed by before. I stop to get something to eat and Google the campground. Hooray! It's just an hour down the road.

The campground is called "Riders Ranch" and when I pull in, a woman with a huge smile greets me. She introduces herself as

Cindy and points to her husband Kirk who's polishing his Harley in the front yard. I call out, "Can I put my bike in the line up? She could use a chrome polish." He laughs and responds, "Not a chance!"

It's a sweet little campground; there are trees and picnic tables and lots of flat grassy spots to set up tents. Cindy says, "After you get unpacked, come on over to the Shelter and have a beer!" Sounds good to me.

The Shelter is large with lots of tables, chairs, couches and a bar. There's rock and roll music playing – and I'm the only guest! Cindy tells me that they have a lot of bikers riding in tomorrow for the long weekend and it will be a party zone, but right now it's quiet. Suits me just fine - I like quiet.

Cindy and Kirk and I sit and drink beer and talk. When they ask me what I do in Vancouver and I tell them I work with special needs kids, Cindy pats Kirk on the back and says, "This is my special needs boy!"

At first I think she's making a joke. But Kirk explains that he had a major speech impediment when he was a kid in Calgary and he went to a Special Needs School from Grade 2 to Grade 8.

Kirk tells me that his Mom, "God bless her," practiced with him every night with flash cards, helping him to pronounce the words slowly and carefully. He credits his Mom and the school he went to for teaching him to talk. When I listen to him speak, there is no trace that he ever had any difficulties.

Cindy says she's going to hit the hay and Kirk calls after her, "Save me a seat." "I always do!" She responds. They're a very cute couple.

Kirk and I have another beer and talk about politics. He is such a red neck but he has a lot of valid points and is very well read. His pet peeve is militant Islam and women wearing burkas. He feels that Canada is about freedom and that if you come here to escape repression in your own country, then don't bring it with you! He's got a sticker on his bike with a Canadian Flag that says, "I'm not racist – I just don't want my country fucked up." OK, so his political perspective is different than mine, but he's got a marshmallow heart towards his wife, kids, grandkids and his three humungous dogs. We call it a night, and even though we haven't solved the world's problems, I've seen them from a different perspective.

DAY 63: September 2
Riders Ranch Motorcycle Campground to
Toad Rock Motorcycle Campground in Balfour, B.C.

In the morning, I hang out in the Shelter where the coffee is ready to go: "Just push the button," Cindy said last night, and I heat water for my oatmeal. Ahhh . . . I sit and relax and write in my journal.

Cindy and Kirk and their gigantic dogs stroll by, "We're just taking our babies for a walk . . . Have you got everything you need?" Cindy calls out. "Yep," I reply. "Just make yourself at home," she says. They're both so friendly and welcoming. I think you have to really enjoy people to run a place like this.

I pack my stuff on my bike, put on my rain gear, (it's not raining right now but it sure looks like it wants to), and warm up Ruby. Cindy comes out from her house and asks if it's OK to take a photo of me for their Facebook page. "Sure!" I say. She gives me a big hug and says, "Next time when you come back, let's go for a ride together – I'll show you some cool places around here!" I'm all for that; it would be fun.

I hit the road and head for the Balfour ferry. I had forgotten how beautiful Hwy 3A is. It's been a long time since Ruby and I have had a chance to dance; you can't dance on the prairies – the road is a straight line. You need curves to dance.

And this road has them . . . just one glorious curve after another, up and down, back and forth with great big Kootenay Lake on my left and forests, mountains, and the occasional small house on my right. It's such a good feeling! Yes! To be dancing again!

And I love riding on roads that lead to ferries; the Balfour Ferry takes about 40 minutes to cross Kootenay Lake. I watch the rain out the window . . . it's warm and dry inside the ferry.

The rain stops when the ferry reaches the other side of the lake – how convenient is that! And it's only a ten-minute ride to Toad Rock; just a short dance with Ruby.

When I pull in, Mary is at the shower house/office/washroom/laundry building. "Hey, Mary! You're back!" she greets me. We laugh together. We've exchanged emails and we both always start them, "Hi Mary," and end them, "From the other Mary." It's our joke together.

Mary is such an amazing person. This is the fourth time I've stayed here over the past three summers. The last time I was with Razz, Wendy and Donna on our way to Glacier Park. It was the July 1st weekend and now its Labor Day weekend. It feels good to have (kind of) started and (almost) ended my journey this summer staying here.

I pick out a campsite with lots of trees because the weather is threatening rain and I know I'm going to want to put my tarp up over the picnic table for some shelter.

I say, "Hi," to the girl next door and introduce myself. Her name is Michelle. There's a big black Harley Ultra Classic parked at her site; I assume she's with a guy and riding two up. Not so – she's riding solo and that's her bike! She said she loves it. She's from Calgary and has been to Toad Rock many times before.

Michelle offers me a beer and invites me over to a campfire a few campsites down with some people she just met. I set up my tent and wander towards the campfire.

Within minutes of sitting down, even though I like Michelle, I realize this really is not my scene. The guys are super drunk and the women are bleached blond with tons of makeup, skimpy tops, and fake tits. One woman goes on and on about how brave Michelle is to travel on her own. She says she would never do that – it's far too dangerous for a beautiful woman to travel alone. (Humility is not her strong suit.) I can't handle this conversation. I finish my beer and excuse myself, saying I need to make dinner.

Over at the cook shack, I heat up some lasagna. There's a pro-
pane stove there and its way easier than unpacking and setting up
my little camp stove. Besides it's starting to rain. I'm thinking I
don't even want to camp here this weekend if my fellow campers
are going to be drunken men and phony done-up women. But
then, in the cook shack, I meet a nice normal couple.

They're dressed in rain ponchos and toques, they're not drunk,
and she is not wearing any make up at all. I like them immediately. We exchange names – He's Roger and she's Sandy. Turns
out they're from Edmonton and they each have their own bikes;
Sandy's got an 05 Sportster and Roger has an Ultra Classic. Roger
pulls their tent trailer behind his bike and they are camping in
style – a full mattress and enough room to stand up in! I'm envi-
ous.

They get along so well, cooking dinner together easily and efficiently. They're warm and friendly and we chat while we share
the covered picnic table and eat. They're both low key and relaxed and real. No phony shit, thank goodness.

I wander down to the Social Pavilion to buy a beer. The Social
Pavilion is a covered area with no walls but it has a bar and a pool
table and lots of couches and comfy chairs. It's a great place to
hang out and meet other campers.

Dan is running the bar. He's a good friend of Mary and Grant and
he comes often to help out and hang out. I met him when I was
here in July. On that occasion he admired Wendy, Razz, Donna,
and my organized campsite. "Ladies, I can tell this is not your first
rodeo!" he said to us.

Dan remembers me and asks about my trip. We chat for a bit
and when I mention that I'm leaving tomorrow he twists my arm;
"You can't leave tomorrow," he says emphatically. "We're having
a party – live music and I'm breaking out the margarita machine!"
I tell him he's a bad influence and he replies, "That what I do best!"

I start talking with a really tall guy who's got the same space
between his two front teeth that my daughter had when she was
growing up. The conversation turns to Chinese astrology and he

mentions that he was born in the year of the Tiger. I say, "I'm the year of the Snake." "1965?" he queries. I laugh. "You're my new best friend – No, 1953." He's surprised. "You're almost as old as me," he says. He introduces himself as Rick and tells me that he and his wife Joyce live in Invermere.

I ask him lots of questions about Invermere and the East Kootenays. It's the next valley east of here and I've never explored that area. He describes it from both a spiritual and geological perspective which is interesting. He explains that the East Kootenay Valley is a transition zone – it's where two plates bumped into each other millions of years ago. That's why the Purcell and Selkirk mountains are smaller than the Rockies; the Rockies are younger mountains and were formed when the plate containing the Purcells and Selkirks bumped into the North American Plate.

Rick tells me that because the East Kootenay Valley is a geological transition zone, the earth in that area has a lot of spiritual energy. He describes a nearby valley, called "Fire Valley," where First Nations peoples have gathered for centuries to perform spirit ceremonies. He says the Indigenous peoples never built villages there. But when white men came, they tried to homestead in the valley. Their homesteads were all destroyed by fire. No loss of life, only material possessions. Today no one lives there; people enjoy hiking in the area and making a spiritual connection with nature.

Good conversation to think about as I wander back to my tent and cozy up for the night.

DAY 64: September 3
Toad Rock Campground

To say it rained hard last night would be an understatement. It's still raining this morning. There is a huge puddle, the size of a small lake, on the road in front of my campsite. Everything is soaked. Thank goodness, I hung a tarp up over my picnic table so I can at least have my usual oatmeal breakfast without getting wet, or rather wetter.

Michelle comes over from next door and we talk. She was planning on leaving today too. We decide that it would be the pits to have to pack up all this soaking wet camping gear and try to load it on our bikes. And besides, if we left today, we'd miss the party! "I'll just have to ride like the wind tomorrow!!" she says. I agree.

I make a couple of phone calls and reserve a cheap motel in Greenwood for tomorrow night. Greenwood is roughly half way to Vancouver from Toad Rock. I figure if I stay in a motel tomorrow night I can get an earlier start on Monday morning than if I camp. I want to hit Hope by early afternoon because traffic in the Fraser Valley will be a gong show with everyone heading home after the long weekend.

I walk down to the Social Pavilion to grab a cup of coffee. Roger and Sandy are there and they're very wet. We're all very wet. It's pouring and its cold and, even though we're wearing rain gear, we're still damp and chilled.

Roger and Sandy said they had started to pack up and realized that it was a dumb idea. Like Michelle and I, they need to be home for work on Tuesday. We are each two days travel distance from our homes – but in different directions: I need to go west, Michelle east and Roger and Sandy ride north. We have all come to the same conclusion: "Ride like the wind . . . tomorrow . . . not today."

That makes it another slow-motion day, my favourite kind! I hang out at the pavilion and chat with various people. Everyone is coming down for coffee and shelter from the rain. The conversation is all about bikes and road trips and good places to go and places to avoid. It's interesting listening to other people's experiences. Theirs usually involves a lot more drinking and mileage per day than mine. But that's alright; there is acceptance among us, each rider "riding their own ride."

Roger and Sandy suggest that since its stopped raining, they're going to head over to Ainsworth Hot Springs for a soak. I enthusiastically agree and we gather our towels and suits and head out.

It's a great curve-filled ride up to the Hot Springs and Roger leads. He's a good solid rider. He's used to riding with Sandy and, like most women (including me), she's slower and more cautious than a guy. Roger knows it and sets a speed that suits our style.

The Hot Springs are packed but we don't care. It just feels good to be warm! There's a big pool that's sort of hot, then there's the caves that are very hot and there's also a small cold plunge pool.

Rick and his wife Joyce are there too and we all chat intermittently. I like Joyce. She works for the school board in Invermere and has a similar job as mine but instead of special needs kids, she works with First Nations children. We talk a lot about how much we enjoy the kids, but that it's the adults (mostly co-workers) who sometimes drive us crazy. She's very spiritual, like her husband Rick, and we share the same beliefs about there being many paths to God.

I like the caves the best and so do Sandy and Roger, and Rick and Joyce. There are mineral deposits encrusted on all the walls and it's dimly lit; you can see just enough to avoid tripping over someone. There's a spot where you can stand and hot mineral water pours out of a crack in the cave wall right onto your back and shoulders. Ahhh!

After a couple of hours, when we figure even our bones are finally warm, we shower and ride back to Toad Rock. It's time to Party!!!

The festivities are in full swing at the Social Pavilion when we arrive. Ron and Dan and Reese are playing guitars and other people are jamming along with bongos, a washboard, and spoons.

Reese has an incredible voice – she's tall and big boned like an Amazon woman with flowing blond hair and, in her own way, she sounds like Janis Joplin. When she sings, it's with her whole heart and soul. She's immersed in the music; she's not really on this planet; she's somewhere off in a universe where it's all about sound.

The Margarita machine hums between songs (so as not to interrupt the music) and bottles of Jack Daniels and Cinnamon Whiskey are being passed around. People are singing along to the choruses and hooting and hollering in appreciation at the end of every song.

I'm not much of a party person but I love the music! I sit with Roger and Sandy on bar stools and sip on my margarita watching the craziness and festivities ebb and flow all around us. I'm enjoying Reese's amazing voice. She sings "Bobby McGee" with so much heart that she transports not just herself to a musical universe, but all the rest of us as well.

The musicians finish and the stereo comes on. Everyone is dancing and singing along. Dan puts on a unicorn head and slow dances with any willing women. It's pretty hilarious! Other masks and headpieces are passed around and the dance floor becomes a menagerie of animals and people, bobbing and dipping in time to the music.

"This is what happens when Hippies get Harleys!" laughs Mary. Yup, I can't help but agree.

DAY 65: September 4
Toad Rock Campground
to Greenwood, B.C.

Very very very slow-motion morning – the whole campground is sleeping. Do ya think that maybe people are a little hung over? Good guess!

Coffee cures anything and gets me and everyone else in motion to pack up our dry (thank goodness) tents and camping gear.

Rick and Joyce are packing too, but Joyce asks me if I would like her to read Tarot cards for me. "I'd love that!" I say enthusiastically. I haven't had a Tarot reading in decades and I like Joyce and trust her.

She shows me her deck which she acquired recently. It's different than a standard Tarot deck – It's called *Animal Wise Tarot* and is based on animal spirits and their attributes.

Joyce asks me to shuffle the deck and to think about a question that I would like answered. I shuffle the cards slowly and carefully, wondering about my purpose in life and thinking about my path.

I hand the deck back to Joyce, she has me cut it, and restack the cards. She explains that she's going to do a five-card reading using the four compass points and then placing the fifth card in the center. She lays the five cards out, placing them face side down.

Joyce turns over the card in the East. It's the 10 of Winged Ones and the picture is of a beautiful Peacock. It says, *Cycle of Death and Resurrection.* Joyce explains that I'm in a cycle of transition right now – that I'm learning lots of new things but that I haven't quite figured out how they all fit together. (That's pretty accurate, isn't it?) She says that the peacock has the ability to spread its feathers and show them to others or to close them so that the colours are unseen. She cautions me about who I show my feathers to - "Not everyone will understand," she says.

Joyce turns over the card in the South and it is the 4 of Four Leggeds. The picture is of a Badger and it says *Self Reliance and Practical Pursuit.* Joyce tells me that I'm a very independent person and that I make my decisions based on practicality. "But," she says, "It's your own version of practicality and not necessarily what other people think is logical or practical." I nod, in my mind this whole trip has been practical: go by myself because guys ride too fast, camp because motels are too expensive, don't plan ahead because the weather changes everything, and don't worry about getting lost because I always seem to end up in good places. It all sounds very practical to me!

The card in the West is the 7 of Shape Shifters. The picture is of a shiny green Beetle and it says *Necessary Decisions for Goals.* The card is reversed when its turned over and Joyce explains that this changes the meaning slightly. She says that I can be very open to group consciousness – that I absorb and internalize the groups mentality and this is not always a good thing for me. I lose my "self" and my own strength. (Interesting, this was also a caution for Reflectors in Human Design). Joyce advises me to be aware of this and that when I am engaged with a group to keep my "self" grounded.

The card in the North is the Queen of Four Leggeds. The picture is of a Lynx and it says *Hidden Knowledge and Creativity.* This card is also reversed. Joyce explains, "You know what you know, Mary Jane. You're solid in your spirituality and you need to remember that. When you feel lost or confused, go back to your gut, your intuition will guide you." We talk about the 6th chakra, the orange one. The mantra is "I love and accept all aspects of myself," Joyce cautions me again, "Like the peacock, don't always show all your feathers. People can sense that you understand more about them than they are revealing."

Joyce explains that the card in the center represents the immediate future. She turns it over. It's the 10 of Four Leggeds. It's a Mother Moose exchanging a kiss with her baby. (Awww, so sweet!) Underneath it says, *Home, Birth, Primal Mother.* Joyce says, "This is your center, who you are meant to be. You are a giver, like Mother Nature, the ultimate giving spirit. You are here to nurture, to support. But like Mother Nature, you must find balance. You have a tendency to give until there is nothing left of yourself. You need to remember to nurture yourself, so that you can nurture others."

Joyce has given me a lot to think about. She thanks me for allowing her to do my reading. That is the definition of a true giver, isn't it? Someone who does something for you and then thanks you for giving them the opportunity. Joyce is a very very special woman.

She and Rick and I exchange big hugs. I know I will see them again. I would love to explore the East Kootenays next summer and have Rick take me to Fire Valley. Their parting words are, "Come see us; you are welcome anytime." I will. I would like to learn more from them.

Ruby and I pull out of Toad Rock and head west. Its already late afternoon but I have that hotel room booked in Greenwood and it's only a few hundred km away. I'll be able to get a good night's sleep and, like Michelle said, "Ride like the wind tomorrow!"

DAY 66: September 5
Greenwood to
North Vancouver, B.C.
Home Sweet Home

I have a great sleep and get up at 6:00 am (Man, that's early!) and on the road by 7:00. I want to get past Hope early enough to avoid the 150-kilometer long parade that will be happening late this afternoon in the Fraser Valley. Its Monday of a long weekend – everybody and their dog will be heading back into Vancouver.

I have to scrape the frost off my motorcycle seat before I can sit on it. "You know its fall when there's frost on the ..." It's so cold I put on my heated vest and plug in.

I take it slow. If there was frost on my seat then, its more than likely, there's frost on the road. There's no traffic at this early hour. I have the road pretty much to myself.

I cruise through Osoyoos. It's a tourist town and the Weekend Winnebagos are awake now and on the road. I don't want to stop and eat in a tourist trap even though I'm really hungry.

I keep riding until Keremeos; it's a little two block long town, just my style and size. It reminds me of many of the small towns that I stopped in across Canada and the U.S. The restaurant is full of local ranchers and I like hearing bits of their conversations about just plain ordinary small-town things.

It occurs to me that today really is my very last day on the road. I'm not sad that the trip is almost over but I'm not happy either to be almost home. I'm feeling satisfied ... satisfied that I had an amazing trip, satisfied that I did it because I wasn't really sure when I started that I could. I say a gratefulness prayer about all the things that I'm thankful for. I feel very blessed.

I ride through the Fraser Valley with hardly any traffic; it was worth getting up early just for that pleasure. I'm enjoying the familiar views, the mountain peaks to the north and south, the mighty Fraser River winding its way through the valley, as I get closer to Home Sweet Home, North Vancouver.

September 5: Evening

It's kind of weird to be home. I like being in my apartment and especially in my cozy bed. My daughter Rebecca is staying with me for a few weeks until she finds an apartment and she is a really good cook! She's stocked the fridge yesterday with all sorts of delicious goodies. Yum!

But reality is going to hit tomorrow. I have to go to work and there is laundry and there will be a list of errands. My life is going to change overnight. But am I a different person now? Have all the experiences in the past two months given me a different perspective on the world? Have I changed on the inside? I think so ... but how that will play out in day to day life, I'm really not sure ... we'll see ...

PART IV: WHAT DID I LEARN FROM THIS JOURNEY?

What do I want to remember?

I want to remember the "Dance" . . . the feeling of effortless flying . . . and to know that it doesn't just apply to riding . . . Life itself is a dance.

That I can do anything I set my mind to - "Believe, conceive, receive."

That I can be myself. It doesn't matter if people think I'm crazy ... they respect me for having the courage to just be me.

Wisdom often comes from unexpected places and people. Be aware and open to receiving it. Sometimes it's an intense conversation with an old friend. Sometimes it's a chance comment from a stranger. Life is a learning adventure. Listen ...

When things go awry between myself and another person, I need to pause and reflect on how I contributed to the situation. (I would prefer to believe it's all their fault!)

When you're doing something huge, break it up into manageable pieces. That way it doesn't feel so scary and overwhelming. And you can pat yourself on the back when you finish a piece.

People have an innate desire to be kind and helpful. It makes them feel good about themselves to "lend a hand" to another human being. Give them the opportunity to assist and then be grateful. It's a Win-Win situation.

Sometimes it's incredible to me how much people love each other (David's story of "my Nita"). They don't seem to see the flaws – they focus on the good stuff.

When you can't change something – accept it – "It is what it is ... "

Family is forever. Friends may come and go overtime. But family is always there. It's a long history of love. They are always part of my life story as I am theirs. It's a forever connection.

"The Power of the Journey." I'm never really sure when I embark on something what the end result will be. I have a plan, an idea but the journey creates itself in the process. Trust that I'm going in the right direction.

The full moon is always a special time for me. Things happen, people appear, events align. Be open and aware.

Remember the welcoming graciousness of Fernando and Anne – homemade Portuguese wine and stories of the Azores. Open with kindness.

When you are in a difficult or dangerous situation, don't just grit your teeth, pull up your bootstraps and power through. Often there's an easier solution ... Think ... maybe there's an alternative.

There are many different paths to God. Everyone is on his or her own spiritual journey and if you listen, they tell you things that help you on your journey. Remember the joy-full laughing Buddha.

If you watch the news, you think people are basically evil. It makes you afraid of others. If you travel, you realize that people are basically good and that they have an innate desire to connect and to share. Spread the love.

How do I end up in exactly the right place after getting lost so many times? Thank you Universe.

I believe that there is hope for mankind when I see what young people are trying to build. Kat's mantra is "Creating a Caring Community." She has a vision of Utopia but at the same time she manifests this vision in reality. The TeaHive is a concrete example.

Inspiration: a gift we give to others and that others give to us.

Synergy: the creation of a whole that is greater than the sum of its parts (4 + 4 = 9 or 10 or 11 ...)

"Life is about the people you meet and the things you create with them, so go out and start creating!"

Be careful what you ask of the universe . . . you just might get it. Raven is a trickster and what he delivers may be what you asked for ... but not necessarily what you wanted.

"Danger" is painted in large letters on the pavement - Don't ignore it. You can feel it in your gut – Don't try to rationalize it away. Pay attention.

Life is a dance of awareness and patience: think of Folleyball at Michel and Claudia's farm. Wait for the moment . . . and then dance when it comes your way.

People are born with certain attributes and challenges. And they are a product of their experience. When you share experiences with someone, you create an emotional connection that increases your understanding of them and yourself.

My favourite roads are the ones where the mountains reach to the sky on one side and the waves caress the shoreline on the other. Zen moments . . .

The object is to hold in your heart the ethics and ideals that are sacred to you and, at the same time, navigate through the real world.

Words of Wisdom from Kat: "Its OK Mom. We all hit ourselves in the face when we're learning!" LOL!

Remember the little crescent shaped beach; how the waves gently break on each end and the crests flow towards each other . . . until they meet with a poufy upward spray of foam and collapse back into the sea . . . together.

"Aren't you just so so so grateful! To be right here, right now!" (Overheard conversation at Future Forest Festival.) Yes, I am "so so so grateful!" especially to the RCMP officers who went out of their way to return my wallet to me. "It's our job to help people," they modestly said. (Maybe, as human beings, that's all our job.)

The only "Self" I have is my own. Stay connected . . .

I love being outside. I love the smell of the wind in my face and the taste of the rain on my lips. I love the forest. I love the ocean. I love falling asleep to the sound of the waves meeting the beach.

Home is where the heart is – Let your heart lead you home.

There are many mentors in your life; your grandparents and your parents play an important role in your early years. Remember the love and the lessons they gave to you.

There's only one God, but so many different pathways to him.

Meditate on the paradox of opposites . . . yin and yang, doing and not doing . . . the effortlessness of being one with the universe.

Remember Austin and Emily and Abby; three kids doing their best in a not-so-great situation. I hope all the love they so readily give comes back to them tenfold.

There's a peacefulness in the prairies . . . it's different than anywhere else. There's a really good feeling about riding toward the horizon. Like your path is laid out.

Life is a combination of destiny and choices. Our destiny is fluid – it changes with the choices we make.

Word of Wisdom from Lisa and Ken: "Our mentality creates our reality."

Words of Love from Kirk and Cindy (before bed): "Save me a seat." "I always do!"

Some opportunities only come once – Seize them! (You can always "ride like the wind" tomorrow).

Let's see if I can integrate the amazing things I've learned into my reality ...

ABOUT THE AUTHOR

Mary Jane Stein

 Mary Jane is an adventurous soul who loves to explore new places and engage with the people she meets as she travels on her intrepid motorcycle Ruby. Mary Jane bought Ruby as a 60th birthday present to herself and has never looked back - except in the rear view mirror to make sure the vehicle following her does not run her over! Feeling blessed to have the freedom to do whatever she wishes every summer, Mary Jane spends the other ten months of the year happily supporting children with Autism in the North Vancouver public school system.

Made in the USA
Monee, IL
11 September 2022